Boodle Boodle Boodle

33 1/3 Global

33 1/3 Global, a series related to but independent from **33 1/3**, takes the format of the original series of short, music-based books and brings the focus to music throughout the world. With initial volumes focusing on Japanese and Brazilian music, the series will also include volumes on the popular music of Australia/Oceania, Europe, Africa, the Middle East and more.

33 1/3 Japan

Series Editor: Noriko Manabe

Spanning a range of artists and genres – from the 1970s rock of Happy End to technopop band Yellow Magic Orchestra, the Shibuya-kei of Cornelius, classic anime series *Cowboy Bebop,* J-Pop/EDM hybrid Perfume, and vocaloid star Hatsune Miku – 33 1/3 Japan is a series devoted to in-depth examination of Japanese popular music of the twentieth and twenty-first centuries.

Published Titles:
Supercell's *Supercell* by Keisuke Yamada
AKB48 by Patrick W. Galbraith and Jason G. Karlin
Yoko Kanno's *Cowboy Bebop Soundtrack* by Rose Bridges
Perfume's *Game* by Patrick St. Michel
Cornelius's *Fantasma* by Martin Roberts
Joe Hisaishi's *My Neighbor Totoro: Soundtrack* by Kunio Hara
Shonen Knife's *Happy Hour* by Brooke McCorkle
Nenes' *Koza Dabasa* by Henry Johnson
Yuming's *The 14th Moon* by Lasse Lehtonen
Toshiko Akiyoshi-Lew Tabackin Big Band's *Kogun* by E. Taylor Atkins

Forthcoming Titles:
Yellow Magic Orchestra's *Yellow Magic Orchestra* by Toshiyuki Ohwada
Kohaku utagassen: The Red and White Song Contest by Shelley Brunt
S.O.B.'s *Don't Be Swindle* by Mahon Murphy and Ran Zwigenberg

33 1/3 Brazil

Series Editor: Jason Stanyek

Covering the genres of samba, tropicália, rock, hip hop, forró, bossa nova, heavy metal and funk, among others, 33 1/3 Brazil is a series devoted to in-depth examination of the most important Brazilian albums of the twentieth and twenty-first centuries.

Published Titles:

Caetano Veloso's *A Foreign Sound* by Barbara Browning

Tim Maia's *Tim Maia Racional Vols. 1 & 2* by Allen Thayer

João Gilberto and Stan Getz's *Getz/Gilberto* by Brian McCann

Gilberto Gil's *Refazenda* by Marc A. Hertzman

Dona Ivone Lara's *Sorriso Negro* by Mila Burns

Milton Nascimento and Lô Borges's *The Corner Club* by Jonathon Grasse

Racionais MCs' *Sobrevivendo no Inferno* by Derek Pardue

Naná Vasconcelos's *Saudades* by Daniel B. Sharp

Chico Buarque's First *Chico Buarque* by Charles A. Perrone

Forthcoming titles:

Jorge Ben Jor's *África Brasil* by Frederick J. Moehn

33 1/3 Europe

Series Editor: Fabian Holt

Spanning a range of artists and genres, 33 1/3 Europe offers engaging accounts of popular and culturally significant albums of Continental Europe and the North Atlantic from the twentieth and twenty-first centuries.

Published Titles:

Darkthrone's *A Blaze in the Northern Sky* by Ross Hagen

Ivo Papazov's *Balkanology* by Carol Silverman

Heiner Müller and Heiner Goebbels's *Wolokolamsker Chaussee* by Philip V. Bohlman

Modeselektor's *Happy Birthday!* by Sean Nye

Mercyful Fate's *Don't Break the Oath* by Henrik Marstal

Bea Playa's *I'll Be Your Plaything* by Anna Szemere and András Rónai

Various Artists' *DJs do Guetto* by Richard Elliott

Czesław Niemen's *Niemen Enigmatic* by Ewa Mazierska and Mariusz Gradowski

Massada's *Astaganaga* by Lutgard Mutsaers

Los Rodriguez's *Sin Documentos* by Fernán del Val and Héctor Fouce

Édith Piaf's *Récital 1961* by David Looseley

Nuovo Canzoniere Italiano's *Bella Ciao* by Jacopo Tomatis

Iannis Xenakis's *Persepolis* by Aram Yardumian

Vopli Vidopliassova's *Tantsi* by Maria Sonevytsky

Amália Rodrigues's *Amália at the Olympia* by Lila Ellen Gray

Ardit Gjebrea's *Projekt Jon* by Nicholas Tochka

Aqua's *Aquarium* by C. C. McKee

Einstürzende Neubauten's *Kollaps* by Melle Jan Kromhout and Jan Nieuwenhuis

J.M.K.E.'s *To the Cold Land* by Brigitta Davidjants

Forthcoming Titles:

Taco Hemingway's *Jarmark* by Kamila Rymajdo

Tripes' *Kefali Gemato Hrisafi* by Dafni Tragaki

Silly's *Februar* by Michael Rauhut

CCCP's *Fedeli Alla Linea's 1964–1985 Affinità-Divergenze Fra Il Compagno Togliatti E Noi Del Conseguimento Della Maggiore Età* by Giacomo Bottà

33 1/3 Oceania

Series Editors: Jon Stratton (senior editor) and Jon Dale (specializing in books on albums from Aotearoa/New Zealand)

Spanning a range of artists and genres from Australian Indigenous artists to Māori and Pasifika artists, from Aotearoa/New Zealand noise music to Australian rock, and including music from Papua and other Pacific islands, 33 1/3 Oceania offers exciting accounts of albums that illustrate the wide range of music made in the Oceania region.

Published Titles:
John Farnham's *Whispering Jack* by Graeme Turner
The Church's *Starfish* by Chris Gibson
Regurgitator's *Unit* by Lachlan Goold and Lauren Istvandity
Kylie Minogue's *Kylie* by Adrian Renzo and Liz Giuffre
Alastair Riddell's *Space Waltz* by Ian Chapman
Hunters & Collectors's *Human Frailty* by Jon Stratton
The Front Lawn's *Songs from the Front Lawn* by Matthew Bannister
Bic Runga's *Drive* by Henry Johnson
The Dead C's *Clyma est mort* by Darren Jorgensen
Ed Kuepper's *Honey Steel's Gold* by John Encarnacao
Chain's *Toward the Blues* by Peter Beilharz
Hilltop Hoods' *The Calling* by Dianne Rodger
Screamfeeder's *Kitten Licks* by Ben Green and Ian Rogers
Soundtrack from *Saturday Night Fever* by Clinton Walker
The Avalanches' *Since I Left You* by Charles Fairchild
The Clean's *Boodle Boodle Boodle* by Geoff Stahl
John Sangster's *The Lord of the Rings, Vols. 1–3* by Bruce Johnson

Forthcoming Titles:
The Triffids' *Born Sandy Devotional* by Christina Ballico
Crowded House's *Together Alone* by Barnaby Smith
5MMM's *Compilation Album of Adelaide Bands 1980* by Collette Snowden
INXS' *Kick* by Ryan Daniel and Lauren Moxey
Sunnyboys' *Sunnyboys* by Stephen Bruel
Eyeliner's *Buy Now* by Michael Brown
Silverchair's *Frogstomp* by Jay Daniel Thompson
TISM's *Machiavelli and the Four Seasons* by Tyler Jenke
The La De Das' *The Happy Prince* by John Tebbutt
Gary Shearston's *Dingo* by Peter Mills

33 1/3 South Asia

Series Editor: Natalie Sarrazin

From the films of Bollywood and Lollywood, to home-grown *bhangra* hip-hop, Hindu devotional pop and Sufi rock, Sri Lankan rap, Indo jazz and disco, new-wave electronica and diasporic Asian Underground scene, 33 1/3 South Asia takes readers on a sonically diverse journey through the most significant soundtracks and albums from the twentieth and twenty-first centuries.

Published:

Dil Chahta Hai Soundtrack by Jayson Beaster-Jones

Lata Mangeshkar's *My Favourites, Volume 2* by Anirudha Bhattacharjee and Chandrashekhar Rao

Forthcoming:

Coke Studio (Season 14) by Rakae Rehman Jamil and Khadija Muzaffar

Boodle Boodle Boodle

Geoff Stahl

Series Editors: Jon Stratton, UniSA Creative, University of South Australia, and Jon Dale, University of Melbourne, Australia

BLOOMSBURY ACADEMIC

NEW YORK • LONDON • OXFORD • NEW DELHI • SYDNEY

BLOOMSBURY ACADEMIC
Bloomsbury Publishing Inc
1385 Broadway, New York, NY 10018, USA
50 Bedford Square, London, WC1B 3DP, UK
29 Earlsfort Terrace, Dublin 2, Ireland

BLOOMSBURY, BLOOMSBURY ACADEMIC and the Diana logo are trademarks
of Bloomsbury Publishing Plc

First published in the United States of America 2025

Library of Congress Cataloging-in-Publication Data
Names: Stahl, Geoff, 1968- author.
Title: Boodle boodle boodle / Geoff Stahl.
Other titles: Clean's Boodle boodle boodle
Description: [1.] | New York : Bloomsbury Academic, 2025. |
Series: 33 1/3 Oceania | Includes bibliographical references and index.
Identifiers: LCCN 2024023548 (print) | LCCN 2024023549 (ebook) | ISBN
9798765106389 (paperback) | ISBN 9798765106372 (hardback) | ISBN
9798765106396 (ebook) | ISBN 9798765106402 (pdf)
Subjects: LCSH: Clean (Musical group). Boodle boodle boodle. | Alternative
rock music–New Zealand–Dunedin–History and criticism. | Rock music–New
Zealand–Dunedin–1981-1990–History and criticism.
Classification: LCC ML3534.6.N44 S73 2025 (print) |
LCC ML3534.6.N44 (ebook) |
DDC 781.660993/9209048–dc23/eng/20240624
LC record available at https://lccn.loc.gov/2024023548
LC ebook record available at https://lccn.loc.gov/2024023549

ISBN: HB: 979-8-7651-0637-2
          PB: 979-8-7651-0638-9
          ePDF: 979-8-7651-0640-2
          eBook: 979-8-7651-0639-6

Typeset by Integra Software Services Pvt. Ltd.
Printed and bound in Great Britain

Series: 33 1/3 Oceania

To find out more about our authors and books visit www.bloomsbury.com and
sign up for our newsletters.

Contents

Acknowledgements

First and foremost, I want to thank David and Hamish Kilgour and Robert Scott for their invaluable contributions to this book and independent music in Aotearoa/New Zealand and beyond.

Thanks also: Roger Shepherd, Richard Langston, Ian Dalziel, Bob Sutton, Carol Tippet and Andrew Shaw for their reminisces; Amanda Mills at the Hocken Collections; William Daymond and Keith McEwing at the Alexander Turnbull Library; Josh Ellery for his research assistance; Jon Stratton for his editorial nous and guiding this book through its various stages; Rachel Moore at Bloomsbury; and the Faculty of Humanities and Social Sciences at Te Herenga Waka/Victoria University of Wellington, Aotearoa/New Zealand.

I'm grateful as well to my friends and colleagues who each offered insights, support, contacts, personal takes, welcome advice and critical commentary, particularly Su Ballard, Michael Brown, Anita Brady, Giacomo Lichtner, Dave Maclennan, Graeme Tuckett, Stephen Norris, Maarten Holl, Mike Hills and Hedwig Eisenbarth.

Introduction: Starting point

In June of 2022, Aotearoa/New Zealand's then prime minister, Jacinda Ardern, travelled across the Tasman to meet up for the first time with the newly elected Australian prime minister, Anthony Albanese.[1] At the obligatory photo-op, the leaders exchanged some of their favourite vinyl LPs. Ardern's swag contained albums from locals Aldous Harding (*Aldous Harding*), Reb Fountain (*Iris*), the reissues of *AK-79*, the classic compilation documenting punk/post-punk from Auckland and The Clean's *Boodle Boodle Boodle* EP (complete with comic insert), originally released in 1981, as well as a couple of Flying Nun Records t-shirts. Albanese swapped out albums from Spiderbait, Powderfinger and Midnight Oil, at which point the New Zealand media righteously proclaimed Ardern the hipper PM in this cordial trans-Tasman battle of leadership cool.[2]

Staged media spectacles aside, *Boodle* stands out from that very laudable stash. No shade on the other LPs, but in *Boodle* Albanese clasped something singular and unique: a cracking NZ masterpiece of DIY music-making. *Boodle* was and remains iconic. It's not wrong to suggest that the Harding and Fountain LPs, even Flying Nun, wouldn't exist without it. *Boodle* and The Clean helped define what it means to make independent music in New Zealand, and, in certain quarters, *Boodle* forms the cornerstone of what became known as indie rock (genre stalwarts Pavement, Yo La Tengo and Superchunk, among many others, cite *Boodle* and the band as an inspiration).[3] Some four decades later, it reverberates as a sonic touchstone, an EP bristling with a spirited buzz that inspired a groundswell of like-minded artists and musicians in early 1980s' Aotearoa. Across its five tracks is etched the urgency and insistence of a creative animus searching for new musical horizons. Its release and ensuing chart success resounded up and down the archipelago, galvanizing like-minded music makers to do it themselves. It is a pivotal record, its cultural impact and legacy outstripping its modest length, a game-changer that shifted the paradigm for music-making in Aotearoa. For many, it is the literal and figurative record of a legendary and definitively New Zealand musical moment, but also, as some would have it, a new New Zealand *sound*. That this sound was emanating not from Auckland, at the time the country's musical centre, but rather Dunedin, a small, unassuming university town on the South Island's lower east coast, with a then-population just over 100,000, was a quirk of geography that only served further to underscore the cultural magnitude of *Boodle*.[4]

Brothers Hamish and David Kilgour, along with Robert Scott, the trio who were The Clean, became *de facto* ambassadors for what was taking shape in Dunedin. It was a city in the late 1970s and early 1980s where a new musical inventiveness was stirring, with an upstart scene starting to draw attention. Here was music-making happening well off the mainstream radar and another world away from what was being heard up north in Auckland. The Clean were making a name for themselves touring the country, touted through word of mouth, on the pages of the music press, through the country's nascent student radio network and, in terms of sales and thus the charts, in record shops. The grassroots hustle was such that their first single, 'Tally Ho!', released in September of 1981 on the fledgling

Flying Nun Records, peaked at Number 19 in the nation's Top 50 and hovered around the charts for six more weeks. That brief stint of triumph was soon to be outdone. Released in November of that same year, *Boodle* entered the singles chart at Number 5 and dropped off in May 1982, making for a remarkable run of twenty-six weeks. By the end of that year, it was the best-selling domestic single in the country. Unprecedented for a record that got zero commercial radio play.

Boodle's chart stamina gave purchase to a home-grown musical transformation that would unfold over the ensuing decades. It unsettled some taken-for-granted notions of the music with which New Zealanders, assumed by many in the mainstream music industry, were otherwise content. The Clean and Flying Nun were not alone in this; other independent labels and artists, locals and non-locals alike, also occupied the charts. Between 1980 and 1981, over thirty-eight post-punk singles and EPs made the Top 50, the majority on small NZ indie labels.[5] This batch of releases, along with *Boodle*, pricked the country's staid musical hegemony, part of a rising tide of home-grown independent, DIY music-making offering an alternative, for fans and bands alike, to the musical status quo.

Boodle, however, stood for something different that set it apart from this new musical uptick. A taut and sonically sundry five-song EP, it draws on a range of influences from the Velvet Underground to The Byrds, Dick Dale, Syd Barrett, Wire, The Stooges, Dylan, PiL, The Kinks and others. It's an alchemy of surf, folk, pop, psychedelia, country and post-punk noise craft. *Boodle*, though, is greater than the sum of these parts. Forged in a crucible fired by DIY pluck, it emerged bristling with an originality that stood out from everything else on the charts (including wares from their independently minded peers). An amalgam of bracing white noise and off-kilter melodic pop, its grooves rattled with ideals and aspirations, a rough and ready dispatch from the South Island foreshadowing that music-making in Aotearoa, independent or otherwise, was about to be irrevocably transformed.

This unexpected chart success gave what The Clean and Flying Nun were doing added leverage. *Boodle's* extended run evidenced that there were music fans out there whose tastes and musical interests didn't align with the glut of safe options populating mainstream radio playlists. Even in a small country like New Zealand, chart hits that defied the usual promotional routes were rare, and a record that charted without radio play only added to its intrigue. That commercial stations remained silent on The Clean further emboldened the band, their fans and the label, helping to ratify their collective awareness that an alternate musical world over which they had a greater say was possible. And that *Boodle* was a hit made it seem much more plausible.

Boodle nudged the lens to focus on what was happening down south in Dunedin. In the late 1970s and 1980s, underground punk and post-punk scenes dotted Aotearoa, mainly in larger cities like Christchurch, Wellington and Auckland. *Boodle* pinned Dunedin to that musical map. Together, these scenes cohered into something subculturally significant: an emerging alternative culture poking and prodding an out-of-touch local music industry. Many of its factions damned that industry even further simply by being indifferent to its formulae. Instead, they turned to their own devices and focused on inventing new ways of doing things, driven by less fiscally focused values and measures of success. Music-making in New Zealand was recalibrating from below, and the country's nascent independent scenes, labels and bands emerged as its new arbiters.

This book considers how it came to be that the *Boodle* EP crystalizes for so many that The Clean were the right band to happen in the right place at the right time. That kind of serendipitous alignment has a magical, ineffable quality that can't be confected or calculated into being. There are melodies and hooks, artful noise, wry humour, exhilarating experimentation and a DIY spryness coursing through *Boodle*. From its hand-drawn cover to the run-out groove, it expressed a sound, style and attitude tuned into the moment. Here is a sensibility pressed into vinyl that resonated with many of those not being served by the kind of culture middle New Zealand had on offer. For this reason, among many others, *Boodle* is an iconic record that speaks for and to a distinct time and place. And not long afterwards, it would extend beyond that, as *Boodle*, The Clean and Flying Nun would give shape, willingly or not, to the myth of the 'Dunedin Sound'.

The emergence and persistence of that myth present a curious cultural phenomenon that invites some probing. What was it about the country's social and cultural context at the time that such a charged aura would coalesce around *Boodle*, Flying Nun Records, and, more so, the 'Dunedin Sound'? What is it about this 'Dunedin Sound' that resonates at the time and still decades later? And not just in Aotearoa, but overseas? In its incipient state, the 'Dunedin Sound' spoke to and for a cultural moment unfolding in a real place with real people. *Boodle*, The Clean and Flying Nun were central players in those heady days, and they helped craft that story. Slowly, over time, it transformed into something outside of and beyond its reference to that reality. In the ensuing decades, it evolved into a myth less *from* or *of* a place and more *about* it, a gloss on a crucial musical moment, the meaning and cultural value of which transcends its origin in the real world. It was laden with increased signifying power but also morphed into a polyvalent phenomenon, useful for some but an affront or annoyance to others.

Myths obscure as much as they elevate, define things and become definitive. They're inclined to foreground select aspects of a story at the expense of others, offering tales told in broad strokes that play up the major characters and downplay the minor ones. This is an orthodox reading of myth, which is in many respects at play here. However, more nuance is possible, such as that offered by semiotician and essayist Roland Barthes. In *Mythologies*, a collection of short, incisive essays focused primarily on the consumer culture of the day (the 1950s), he reminds us that myths do not hide; instead, they make themselves seen (and heard).[6] They are refined to purity in their ostentation, disavowing inconsistencies that might otherwise complicate things and presenting a preferred view of the world instead. In this sense, they also arrogate for themselves a blissful clarity, lifting events and things out of their origins in the world of social relations, of historical and material circumstance, (re)presenting them as ahistorical, asocial, universal and imbued with the unassailable character of 'statements of fact'. They become floating signifiers, a cluster of meanings and associations divorced from their reference point, functioning as neither 'a lie nor a confession', Barthes suggests, but rather as 'an inflexion'.[7] These formations, in this sense, are also deformations but are now endowed with social and cultural power.

To that end, revealing the truth or falsity of a myth is not so much the point, though it's right to question how it came to be. In deciphering myths, and because they are about social and cultural power and their inflexions, we should look at how they come to mean what they do, to whom and whose or what interests are served. The media are essential here, as they help myths work by doing the work of myth. As mechanisms of inflexion, they play a critical role in manufacturing myths and framing and packaging them into neat, easily digestible forms, a convenient morselization that aids their circulation through a culture. Myths are eloquent abstractions that can stand for things, reflect and refract back to us a *précis* of events that happened in the real world. In the case of the 'Dunedin Sound', this is a myth that, over decades, wended its way through a tangle of media, from zines to magazines, radio and television, to websites and archives, moving from margin to mainstream. Media at the time serviced and reproduced the myth and continue to underwrite its persistence today. Keeping this in mind, the aim is not to explode or dispel the myths surrounding the 'Dunedin Sound'. Instead, consideration of The Clean, *Boodle* and Flying Nun offers different lenses for thinking through the mechanics at work, what's at stake, and for whom, as well as its varied inflexions in telling this story.

Much like elsewhere, storytelling plays a vital role in New Zealand. It's fundamental to how different communities and constituencies understand and live their experience of place. Whose stories get told and who tells them are central to the country's identity. There are founding and foundational tales, such as Māori legends, myths and oral traditions (*pūrākau*), as well as colonizer stories and myths, both tying people to Aotearoa in very different, uneven, sometimes competing, sometimes complementary ways. Myths have their use and continue to be useful to this very day. They can insinuate people into a unique relationship with a place, remind them of where they come from and their duty of stewardship towards that place and its people. They facilitate ways of knowing and being by relating the past to the present and the future. These myths come from below and reflect the affective affinities between people and places. Myths may also function with a degree of political expediency, working in the service of hegemony, as Barthes suggests, privileging narratives that reiterate the interests of one group over others. We could say these emanate from those in power and, in this capacity, have an added ideological bent. In Aotearoa, the affective and ideological dimensions of myths are continually at play, forming the country's meaning and mattering maps and animating the *kōrero* (conversation) around the complexities of this place. To talk of myth is hardly out of place here; it is very much *of* this place.

Music-making has a propensity towards mythmaking. In its social forms (scenes and subcultures), its material culture (LPs, CDs, cassettes, memorabilia), the media industries and institutions that promote and preserve it (zines, radio, TV, record labels, digital platforms, museums, archives), the places that give it life (cities, suburbs, towns, bedrooms, rehearsal spaces, studios and performance venues) and the very people that make it (artists, producers, engineers, label owners, managers and impresarios), music-making offers a rich assortment of ingredients ripe for mythmaking. With that in mind, the tale's various tellers and keepers are the voices drawn from for this re-presentation of *Boodle*, The Clean, Flying Nun and the 'Dunedin Sound'. This includes interviews done at the time and afterwards, from in-person conversations and correspondences, as well as the countless media delineations found in zines, magazines, documentaries, news stories, blogs, websites, archives and more, all of which have given the myth its appealing striations and troubled variegations. These sit alongside contemporary reflections, memoirs and overviews that add additional valence to the myth. In referring to *that* myth, some music-makers and critics use 'myth' as an epithet, while others see some merit in it. Many of these storytellers are frank about where they stand in relation to it, ranging from the reverential to the resentful and many shades between. And, of course, this book, too, adds another layer to the myth.

Boodle still bears a semantic force that has hardly dimmed in the four decades since its release; in fact, this has only been enhanced, its patina deepened by the stories still told about it. Alongside Flying Nun, *Boodle* carries a great deal of musical and cultural heft, a phenomenon that mattered then and matters now. Over the years, however, what that mattering means has shifted in complex, fraught and convoluted ways. This book aspires to parse out some of these meanings and matterings, exploring how a myth that shadows *Boodle*, The Clean and Flying Nun, took (and mistook) its place in Dunedin, New Zealand (and elsewhere).

Chapter 1, 'Back in the day', sets the scene by sketching out the larger context in New Zealand in which The Clean and *Boodle* emerged, looking more closely at Dunedin and a nascent music scene on the cusp of a new decade. Chapter 2, *'Boodle Boodle Boodle'*, delves into the EP itself. It explores the songs and the unique circumstances of their making, from the recording space, the soon-to-be legendary four-track recorder, the quick two-day recording session and the EP's curious title and distinctive packaging. Chapter 3, 'Aftermath', considers the broader impact of *Boodle* following its release, its chart success and how it catalysed Flying Nun, other bands in Dunedin and the budding independent scenes taking shape around Aotearoa. Chapter 4, 'Great sounds great', maps the origins of the 'Dunedin Sound', with The Clean held up at first as emissaries and later icons. This segues into Chapter 5, 'Trapped in amber', a consideration of how the myth that marries the

Dunedin Sound, The Clean and Flying Nun, functions as a complex legacy for the city. The final chapter, 'Do your thing', serves as a coda, circling back to The Clean to engage with their legacy and habit of playing outside the rules.

This book also plays outside the rules in its own way. *Boodle* is not an album; it's an EP [extended play] and classed as a single. And it plays at 45 rpm, not your standard LP speed of 33 1/3. With a total playing time of just over sixteen minutes, it's only five tracks and one of those clocks in at 5 minutes and 30 seconds. The Clean did release LPs, though their first proper album, *Vehicle* (Rough Trade), came out in 1990, a decade after they first started playing together. While unquestionably The Clean, focusing on *Vehicle* would require telling a different story. This book suggests that when *Boodle* arrived, it *did* things, had *consequences*. Its impact was immediate and its influence ongoing, with The Clean, *Boodle Boodle Boodle* and Flying Nun entwined in the country's cultural matrix and more so its national identity through the myriad stories that have been, and continue to be, told about it. Of which this is (yet) another.

1   Back in the day

1981 was a busy, pivotal time. The right-wing National government was in power and had invited the racially selected Springbok Rugby team to tour NZ, this split the country in two and there were huge anti-tour marches at each match venue, we were touring the country at the same time and joined the anti-tour protest in Auckland, it was very violent and a real eye opener. — **ROBERT SCOTT**[1]

1981 offers a critical vantage point from which to consider the state of Aotearoa and its complex social, cultural and political milieu. For many, the year was unmistakably grim, a view that hints at how and why *Boodle* resonated in the way it did (and does). Several economic and social issues that had been roiling in New Zealand's recent past were playing out in increasingly visible and visceral ways, bringing to a boil long-simmering resentments and demands for real social and cultural change. How these were manifest would see the country indelibly, irrevocably altered. *Boodle* is a sonic memento allied to that time, expressing a communal sentiment etched in vinyl. In this, it was but one, albeit a significant, herald of what some of that change might look and sound like.

From the mid-to-late 1970s, there was deepening economic uncertainty due to then Prime Minister Robert Muldoon's freezing of wages and prices, stagflation and the protectionist and populist policies that stultified the country. These sat alongside ongoing and increasingly aggravated race relations, signalled on a larger scale by Māori-led protests such as the peaceful *hīkoi* (land march) in 1975 that highlighted the disenfranchisement from native land, starting in Te Hāpua at the very top of the North Island moving along State Highway 1 to Parliament grounds in the capital Wellington, swelling to over 5,000 people along the way.

Not long after the *hīkoi*, that deepening resentment among Māori erupted violently following the government's brutal confiscation in 1978 of land at Takaparawhau/Bastion Point. The land was seized to be redeveloped for luxury housing, taken from the Māori hapū Ngāti Whātua Ōrākei, who, in protest, had occupied the land for over 500 days before being forcibly removed. This is a cursory sample of the type of top-down governmental action and bottom-up resistance that, for some, had brought Aotearoa to the precipice, if not an existential brink. More pointedly, there were determined calls among an increasing number of Māori, Pākehā and others for real substantive change.[2]

Outside the cage

1981 is a salient period to consider some visible and audible exemplars gesturing towards what that change might look like. The way forward was signposted by several social and cultural disruptions and eruptions that shaped a national reckoning. Some of these events occurred on a scale that forced a confrontation with the settler nation's past (and present) status as a colonial outpost of the British Commonwealth. Others pointed towards an emergent space of possibility, allowing for some a way to reimagine New Zealand's future as a bicultural nation-state deeply connected to Oceania, on the cusp of taking on the mantle of an outward-looking nation focused on the region and, more so, the world. These glimmers of hope played out in the public arena to varying degrees and on different scales.

One of those glints was shimmering on the silver screen, with a local film industry gaining a deeper toehold in the nation's imagination. 1981 saw the release of *Goodbye Pork Pie*, directed by Geoff Murphy, a foray into the road movie genre and Aotearoa's first locally made box-office hit. Described by *Variety* at the time as '*Easy Rider* meets the *Keystone Kops*', nearly a sixth of the population saw it and was the first domestic film to break $1,000,000 in ticket sales.[3] Some viewed *Pork Pie* as a tipping point, after which Aotearoa/New Zealand's film industry was deemed worthy of telling its own stories through its storytellers to an appreciative and supportive audience and with an ever-diminishing cultural cringe.

Widening the pop culture catchment, one of the year's breakthrough musical hits was Auckland-based Blam Blam Blam's 'There is No Depression in New Zealand' (Propeller Records, 1981), a tongue-in-cheek piss-take on the 'she'll be right' stereotype of the laid-back 'Kiwi', and the all-too-cosy 'blokeism' that oozed out of Muldoon and his cronies in power. Released on the indie upstart Propeller Records, the song ventriloquizes a litany of the denialisms from those who held cultural and economic sway, a catalogue of complacencies of a large segment of New Zealand wilfully ignoring what's in front of them. 'We have no dole queues, we have no drug addicts, we have no racism, we have no sexism, sexism, no, no', they sarcastically chanted. Released in July of 1981, the song's poking and prodding of an un-reflexive jingoism was prescient, intoning 'there is no unrest in this country', and it was shortly to become the *de facto* anthem for a long-simmering resentment that in August was about to violently boil over courtesy of the country's cherished national sport, rugby.

The spark for this nationwide tumult was the Springbok Tour, which saw the South African rugby team take on their New Zealand rivals, the All Blacks, in a series of matches held across the country. As it was still under the apartheid regime, many other countries had banned travel to South Africa to compete or denied the Springboks entry to play locally. However, Muldoon, ever the populist, insisted on allowing the tour to go head, set to run from July to September. The result was protests up and down the country, involving many thousands of people, Māori and Pākehā and others, which, at times, the police attacked ferociously.[4] There were countless bloody confrontations, many of which made the evening news and front pages, as police beat protesters with their recently acquired batons, a violent, new method of crowd control. Matches were interrupted or cancelled outright as rugby pitches were overrun with police, protesters, fans, placards and smoke bombs. Over those three months, the country was wracked by large-scale civil unrest that drove a wedge between rural and urban, young and old, and Māori and Pākehā, but also mobilized new social and political alliances, the consequences of which would reverberate for years, decades, afterwards.[5]

Before the dust had even time to settle after the disastrous Springboks Tour, there came a piquant reminder for this settler nation of the trauma of its colonial tether. In October that same year, Queen Elizabeth II undertook a short tour of Aotearoa, including a Dunedin stop. At the time, a minor crime spree was unfolding, perpetrated by seventeen-year-old Christopher John Lewis and some friends who had formed the National Imperial Guerrilla Army. They threatened to continue 'to steal, rob or even kill … unless if the Springbok team leaves

New Zealand', tapping into the current national mood.[6] The Queen was scheduled to visit Dunedin's Otago Museum. Lewis took a rifle and rode his bike to the Adams Building at the neighbouring Otago University, where, from a toilet cubicle five storeys up, he attempted to assassinate her. He fired and missed. Upon his arrest, Lewis claimed that his intent in trying to take out the Queen was to bring attention to the numerous issues the country was facing. Tellingly, the attempt on the Queen's life was only revealed to New Zealanders in 2018, when documents related to the incident were released to the media. Police and authorities feared making it public at the time might have meant an end to royal tours, leading to a decades-long suppression that further kowtowed to the country's monarchical ties.

This international incident, which wasn't an international incident, or even a national one for that matter, secreted away for nearly four decades, stands as a parable. It tells the story of parts of a nation still in thrall to the myth of colonialism in the face of long-simmering resentments against the Queen and country now erupting across the archipelago. The status quo would no longer do. What happened in Dunedin crystallizes so many of the issues that were seizing the country at the time, and, in a fashion, the city was emerging as a barometer. It shaped what Raymond Williams calls a 'structure of feeling'.[7] It's a concept that goes some way to contextualizing how preferred world views might be challenged by new ways of being, thinking and doing, and how the latter manifest, as one avenue, in cultural texts (he's pointing to literature primarily, but it applies as well to music and other texts). The use of 'feeling' is essential as it refers to an affective state or collective sentiment that has not yet settled into anything coherent or purposeful, let alone fully formed. It's an idea focused on a sense of emergence, particularly around ideas or forms of expression that might challenge prevailing ideologies and posit alternative moral universes. As these are only just coming into view and thus have not yet been consecrated as art, their quotidian dimensions allow them to resonate prosaically yet potently. In coming from the people, from 'below' as such, they reiterate Williams's claim that 'culture is ordinary', placing them in stark contrast to top-down notions of culture that privilege elitist ideals.[8] 'Structure of feeling' speaks to this as a conceptual prism for contemplating how some of those cultural and social shifts in Aotearoa at the time manifest across literature, art, film and music, positioning them as anchor points to which different narratives (and myths) could be hitched. In thinking about cultural forms in their historical circumstance, 'structure of feeling' offers a framework to consider how they acquire their power in speaking to and from, for and against, the broader context of their making. In the case of Dunedin, given its history and place in the New Zealand imaginary, the city served as an ideal incubator for particular sentiments to take hold, shaping a unique sociomusical experience. This made new and different sorts of musical practices possible and gave way to the distinctive sound and its attendant ethos emerging in the late 1970s and early 1980s.

At the bottom

Ōtepoti/Dunedin is a city that holds a distinctive place in the New Zealand imaginary due to its geographical and historical circumstances, both of which made possible The Clean and what they came to stand for musically and culturally. Located on the lower east coast of New Zealand's South Island, the city sits at the southern end of a natural harbour formed by the Otago Peninsula. The distinctive topography surrounding the city results from a rich geological history shaped by millennia of volcanic eruptions, sedimentation and coastal erosion. These folded and faulted rock layers give rise to the city's hilly terrain, valleys and dramatic coastline. The unique topography also lends the city its notoriously cold and damp winters.

The early settlement of Ōtepoti has a complex history that includes both Māori and Europeans (among others). The area was visited by travellers and explorers from Polynesia as early as the tenth century, and permanent settlements roughly dated back to about the twelfth century. These early original settlers, now identified as Māori, asserted a way of life very quickly, and from them we get the name Ōtepoti ('place situated at a corner'). A migration from the North Island saw Kāi/Ngāi Tahu become the dominant group on the South Island. Māori *iwi* (tribes) and *hapū* (clans) continue to have a profound cultural and historical connection to the region, its land and its natural features, which form the foundation of their oral traditions and mythologies.

Permanent European settlement in the region began in the early nineteenth century. These were groups drawn to the area, like Māori, for its rich maritime resources, primarily seals and whales. In 1848, the evangelical Free Church of Scotland, which had seceded from the Church of Scotland, sent a group of settlers, led by William Cargill, to secure a new Scottish Presbyterian community in the South Island. They established the city of Dunedin, so-called after the Scottish Gaelic name for Edinburgh, 'Dùn Èideann'. They purchased land from the Kāi Tahu iwi through Te Tiriti o Waitangi/The Treaty of Waitangi and established the city on the shores of Otago Harbour (the 'purchase' of land by the Crown across the country, and the consequent alienation of Māori from it, after the signing of Te Tiriti in 1840 laid the foundations for the symbolic and very real violence of the past and present of colonialism in Aotearoa).[9] This new wave of colonizing settlers brought their architecture, farming, customs and culture, and educational ideals. The latter included the founding of Aotearoa's first art school (the Dunedin School of Art, in 1870) and the country's first university, the Gothic-inspired Otago University (established in 1869, co-founded by the Scottish poet Robbie Burns's nephew, Thomas Burns). The city's built landscape, as well as its social and cultural life, was indelibly shaped by these institutions.

The discovery of gold in the Tuapeka River in Central Otago in 1861 led to a rush, the country's biggest, peaking around 1863. The region consequently changed dramatically, as did Dunedin, as thousands of miners from around New Zealand and overseas (primarily China) flocked there to seek their fortune. Gold drove the New Zealand economy then, and Ōtepoti was where many panhandlers, miners and their families settled to live and process their hauls. For a moment, it had the most significant urban population in Aotearoa. Hotels, restaurants, commercial buildings and residences appeared quickly to accommodate this, including several public houses, which became essential institutions for the city's social and cultural life as the rush took hold. Among these establishments were The Queen's Arms (est. 1848, just before the rush; rebuilt on the same site in 1879), which would change its name to The Empire Hotel (1898), the Crown Hotel (est. 1862) and the Captain Cook Hotel (est. 1864; later the Captain Cook Tavern). All would serve as crucial music venues in the late 1970s and early 1980s, some hosting the new wave of Dunedin bands.

Of these, the Empire is often seen as the most significant. In the upstairs bar, The Clean headlined the first rock gig held in 1981, supported by The Verlaines (door charge 50 cents). Shortly after, the Empire became the *de facto* home of the 'Dunedin Sound'.

Different world

Pubs and taverns like the Empire, the Cook and the Crown remained long after the gold veins had dried up, monumental remainders in, and reminders of, a city once at the heart of the country's economy. As Dunedin edged into the twentieth century and continued to lose its lustre, it acquired another character, a present haunted by its many pasts, as Jennifer Lawn suggests:

> (A) combination of religious protest, colonial idealism, commercial wealth, and subsequent slow decline. The gold rush boom of the 1860s could not be sustained, and over the next century the northward evacuation of capital left many of the city buildings untouched by (m)odern architecture, making Dunedin a living Victorian and Edwardian cityscape signifying, not the ebullience of empire, but decay and the gravity of time.[10]

For Lawn, Dunedin is a city burdened with a solemnity tied to a declining majesty and the trauma of its settler-colonial history. While that narrative predominantly tells a story of economic withering, from another angle, those failures also fostered spaces that allowed a counterculture to stake a claim in the city. Erik Olssen, in his history of Otago, suggests that by the 1970s,

Dunedin's diminished fortunes, leaving a town foundering in some eyes, had a contrary positive effect. In a waning economy, some saw 'a vantage point from which individuals could distance themselves from the deeper obsessions and hungers expressed in New World materialism and the ideology of consumption'.[11] He suggests it's still a conservative city 'dominated by Presbyterians', but this is tempered, 'profoundly shaped by Calvinism and non-conformity'.[12] However tiny or niche, Dunedin has space for progressive ideas and ideals beneath the conventional orthodoxy that otherwise tends to be its public face.

This tension plays out in Dunedin's cultural spaces in consequential ways. The new music scene of the late 1970s took its place in a city grappling with those twinned forces of conservativism and non-conformity, the former dominating the latter, an uneven ratio that further goaded music-makers into insisting on doing things differently. Being a university town, a place where writers and artists of note were born, settled or frequented (such as Janet Frame, Hone Tuwhare, Peter Olds, Ralph Hotere, James K. Baxter and Sam Hunt, among others), and with a resilient and long-standing musical culture running through church groups and community halls, there was (and is) a strain of creative and attendant bohemian life that thrived in pockets of the city. A few local bands made their mark not long before then, including the In-Betweens and Lutha in the early part of the decade, and by the mid-1970s, Mother Goose made a name for themselves and the city (though they made the standard move to Australia to seek greater success).[13] In other words, The Clean did not appear in a musical or cultural void. However, their unconventional sound took time to find a foothold. Dunedin in the late 1970s was not an easy place to make music that didn't fit the mould. As many musicians at the time attest, it was rife with violence against anyone who looked or sounded different. However, that very visceral scenario gave what The Clean and their musical peers were doing a more pronounced, almost existential, necessity.

Filling a hole

David and Hamish Kilgour hail from Ranfurly, a farming town in Central Otago, just over 100 km north of Dunedin. They grew up around farms in rural regions in those early years, moving to Dunedin when David was about ten. A few years later, the brothers started making music in their bedroom. David recalls their 'influences were many and were driven by being children of the 60s and 70s'.[14] Their mother sang and played piano and had a collection of records that included the likes of Harry Belafonte, Hank Williams, Chopin, Liberace, Dinah Lee, Burl Ives, and local country star John Hore. 'Plus', he adds, 'the radio or gramophone was never far away, so add in what the radios were blasting at the time'.[15] These were the kinds of musical influences and atmospheres that piqued the brothers' interests in making music of their own, which only increased as they got older and found themselves out and about in Dunedin and trying to tap into the city's creative culture, however meagre it might have seemed at the time.

Silence or something else

Being creative in Dunedin was hardly a straightforward option. David recollects that 'a life of the arts was discouraged, even scoffed at. What (poet) Sam Hunt was up against here in NZ in the 60s was, as Sam says, "hard going at times".[16] There were, however, hints of an alternate universe. Hamish recalls there were a few spaces, art classes and later art school, for example, where creative types could find their footing in a bohemian side of the city that prompted visions of another way of life:

> We had a cool art teacher, we did photography, sculptures for a small ceramic kiln and we'd be listening to radical socialist schoolteachers talking about Malthus, playing us 'Revolution No.9', digging Hendrix, Joe Cocker, The Who, The Stones, Led Zeppelin, The Byrds, Jim Morrison's lyrics.[17]

There was another world out there. It was a small space, but it had a voice, however marginalised it was. Ōtepoti was the home of *The Counter Culture Free Press* (est. 1972), which did what it said on the tin: an irreverent publication but one that also took quite serious stands on queer, feminist and other civil rights issues.[18] It was an essential medium for Dunedin's (and New Zealand's) countercultures, making space to model a different way of life and challenge the status quo. That a tiny sliver of unconventional living could be found in staid, conservative Dunedin, recesses where a bohemian life took hold and creative types could find themselves and like-minded others, was crucial to getting by.

And, like so many others around the world at the time, punk music prodded the Kilgours to turn that niche into a thing, grabbing some instruments and making noise together. 'The whole content over style (three chords not twenty!) and DIY approach especially was a big influence,' David recalls, where 'the attitude was almost as important than the music at times but of course both fed into each other'.[19] Thus, in 1978, they put a band together in that very spirit of punk. Being surfers, Hamish and David were inspired by the character Mr. Clean (played by Charles Dierkop) in the surfer/biker flick *The Sweet Ride* (Harvey Hart, 1968) and settled on The Clean.

The Clean's first incarnation had Hamish on the drums, while David played guitar, and his school friend Peter Gutteridge joined in on bass and sang as well. Shortly afterwards, they brought Doug Hood to the front as the singer for their first live sets. They supported recently anointed punk icons The Enemy at a local venue, The Old Beneficiaries Hall. The gigs were legendarily shambolic. David noted they were memorable for what The Clean wasn't: a cohesive unit, though they had an indefatigable DIY zeal that triumphed over their lack of musical chops. Roy Colbert, who ran the local record shop, Records Records, and also wrote for the free national music magazine *Rip It Up*, said of the first of those early sets, it 'was yer definitive rock'n'roll cock-up false starts, forgotten words, unintentional key changes, ignored cues, the lot, all of it linked by David Kilgour's white noise guitar and brother Hamish's magnetisation to the snare drum'.[20] David concurs, with plenty of haters at those early shows in Dunedin: 'The Clean couldn't play at all. We couldn't play our instruments at all. And The Enemy supposedly had some sort of rough idea of what they were doing. But the whole concept of what we were doing, didn't know what we were on about. They said go away, come back next year or whatever'.[21]

Stomp the guru

The Enemy. They were crucial figures in those early days, the band riding roughshod over complacency and boredom. They formed in 1977, with Alec Bathgate on guitar, Mick Dawson playing bass, Mike Dooley handling drums, and fronted by Chris Knox, who sang (Hamish Kilgour had tried out for drummer but wasn't fond of Knox's dominance). The Enemy (a play on the UK music weekly the *NME*) had their first set in November of that year at the Old Beneficiaries Hall, which was ground zero for what was unfolding. With the charismatic Knox as their singer, The Enemy set underground Dunedin alight with their confronting live shows, which thrilled (and challenged) the punters with a punk-inspired charge.[22] They were inspired by bands like the MC5 and The Stooges, and it showed. Knox had adopted Iggy's habit of cutting himself live on stage in a visceral act of fealty (a tribute paid during performances of their song 'Iggy Told Me'). They quickly gained notoriety, being the only band of its sort in town, and their bastardized translation of punk jolted a new music scene into being.

Knox acknowledges that punk played out differently in Dunedin, noting there weren't any apparent punks in town, 'just people who went along to these gigs. Because down in Dunedin, there was already a sort of vague counterculture, and bands like The Enemy and The Clean gave it a bit of focus. But it never really became a real punky thing. The idea of becoming a punk was pretty well sneered upon.'[23] Their influence was audible, and they established a common ground that was not only sonic but revelled in its difference from the mainstream. 'You can hear The Enemy in the Chills, The Verlaines and most notably The Clean', says Knox. 'They all had the same aims and the same problem: Where do you play if you're not middle-of-the-road?'[24] The band's sound and style were far from what most of the local punters were used to, which kept them marginalized and fending for themselves. The Clean found them kindred spirits. David, echoing Knox, recalls that 'The Clean and The Enemy weren't really known as a middle-of-the-road band …. We had to organise our own gigs, and it started with The Beneficiaries [Hall] at first and The Coronation Hall'.[25]

Slowly starting to array around The Clean were people who would become prominent figures in their story and, more so, the myth of the 'sound'; a phenomenon that the band and their peers would soon be caught up in. Doug Hood was one, Chris Knox another. Chris was a motivating, if sometimes divisive, figure in the scene, fashioning himself a subcultural custodian, offering bands pointed advice about good and bad songs or gigs, often whether or not they wanted it. Hailing originally from Invercargill, New Zealand's southernmost city, Knox moved to Dunedin for university in the early 1970s. He and Hood were roomies there, based at Filluel Street, which in the late 1970s was becoming a hub for the burgeoning scene. Chris was a bit older than those who would become his musical peers in the late 1970s, but musically, and some might say spiritually, he became something of a mentor to and cheerleader for many of the up-and-coming bands.

After a brief stint in town, The Enemy left Ōtepoti to wade into the Auckland/Tāmaki-Makaurau scene. However, by the end of 1979, Mick Dawson had gone, and the band was effectively over. Knox, Bathgate and Dooley appeared with a new outfit while there, Toy Love, joined by Paul Kean (bass) and Jane Walker (keyboards). Doug Hood served as their live sound engineer and *de facto* manager. Much more of a new-wave band, Toy Love put out a few singles that managed to chart, accompanied by some very humorous videos, decamped across the ditch to Sydney, where they recorded an eponymous album for WEA, immediately got disillusioned with major label demands, returned to Aotearoa, did a final national tour and then disbanded. For Knox, this mundanely rote rock'n'roll story morphed into a cautionary tale about selling out, the moral of which was not to cross the ditch (i.e. the Tasman Sea). It was his stock-standard advice to many of the new Dunedin bands, and a fair few believed it. Hamish said of that tale: 'You can only learn from Toy Love … they tried to be as idealistic as possible and they tried to be honest. They did their best and they got chewed up by the business, and that's an example to any band'.[26] Knox's sway was such that parochialism became a badge of local pride, the key to keeping things authentic, and authenticity would become one of the central tenets of the myth starting to gather around the Dunedin scene.

On again/off again

Hamish takes up the story: 'After The Enemy left town, there was a complete vacuum for a long time. We played and played and wrote lots of good songs, "Point That Thing" was one, but no-one was interested. We were considered musically shocking at that point'.[27] Hood wasn't much on the mic, so his stint in the band was brief (Doug remains central to the band's story, shortly to become more important as a producer and engineer for The Clean, among many others). Lindsay Hooke joined in on drums, and Hamish took on vocal duty. Not long after this, Peter was asked to leave due to, in Hamish's affectionate characterization, 'lagging behind in terms of his application to the bass'.[28] The Clean then left Ōtepoti, having gotten 'sick of organising our own dances as the only places to play', Hamish claimed.[29]

Heading up to Tāmaki-Makaurau to join Toy Love in 1979, the band entertained a rotating cast of bassists, none of whom stuck around for long (included here was Jessica Walker, sister of Toy Love's Jane Walker, and who would join Shoes This High, which made their name in Wellington's artier music scene). The Clean's northern sojourn was short, playing only a handful of gigs before disbanding. Hamish lingered around Auckland and got on board with local outfit The SOBS (Sons of Bitches). David returned to Dunedin and joined The Stains, though he shortly met up with Robert Scott, whom he knew through art school and was flatting with David's girlfriend.

Robert had arrived from East Taieri, near Mosgiel, about 15 km from Dunedin. He also came from a musical household. His dad was a sax player in a Scottish dance band in the 1950s, his mom a pianist, and he was surrounded by Scottish folk music, which informed much of his feel for melody. He took up the piano and the trumpet and taught himself guitar, 'playing along to Neil Young and Bob Dylan LPs from my sister's record collection'.[30] Scott also learned the bass, inspired by his attendance at one of the first Enemy/Clean gigs. With those musical chops and references as an amenable pedigree, he and David started jamming and writing songs together. When Hamish returned from Auckland, The Clean was rebooted, underway again in what Robert recalls as 'a wonderful productive time'.[31] Henceforth, this would be the core trio The Clean would remain for over three decades.

Too much violence

Auckland was relatively flush with punk and post-punk outfits making music in the late 1970s (encapsulated on the Ripper Records comp, *AK 79*, the same album Ardern passed on to Albanese), though by the early 1980s, this was starting to fade. Dunedin wasn't nearly as robust, but things were simmering. Between The Clean's time up on the North Island and their new incarnation down south, bands such as The Stones, The Same (soon to be The Chills) and The Verlaines cropped up, among a couple of others, all of which made for good musical allies and gave the scene added weight. And it felt as though the musical centres of gravity were starting to shift from north to south, also supported by an active scene asserting itself in the southern city's neighbour just to the north, Ōtautahi/ Christchurch.

It still wasn't easy, however. In Dunedin, the revamped band were up against it from the start, having to make a go of it in a city still known, as Hamish referred to it, as 'a right little conservative shit hole – still is to a degree'.[32] A violent undercurrent coursed through the city's social and cultural life, and if you didn't fit in, you risked suffering all manner of abuse. At the time, Hamish recounted, 'I have been punched walking along the street for wearing different clothing. Punk bashing used to be a hobby of Dunedin car boys …. I think we always had the feeling we were bashing our heads against a brick wall'.[33] Gigs occasionally ended in fistfights with local skinheads and police callouts. Graeme Downes, of new allies The Verlaines, recalls that violence was very much part of the social fabric in the city, 'a big thing in our lives at that time', he recalls. 'There was a lot of scarfie [student] bashing, punk bashing and with the Springbok tour, bashing of anyone who was anti-tour. To the fluffy-dice, Valiant-driving bogans that would lie in wait at midnight outside the public gigs where bands like The Clean played, we were all three'.[34] David shares a similar take, taking solace in the fact that with some success came a desire to soldier on, despite the physical threats, carving out a space in Ōtepoti by not giving in to the violence. 'We were up against it here in Dunedin until we had the success with *Boodle* really', he recalls, so in some ways (it was) artistically stifling for us but also made us more resolute. Culturally speaking we were still dealing with a very conservative New Zealand, but in saying that some say Dunedin and perhaps other parts of New Zealand are more forgiving of their freaks and allow them their space. I think this rings true of Dunedin in some ways to this day still.[35]

The Clean were committed to the cause of tolerance for those countercultural types who then (and still) had a hard time of it in Aotearoa. Hamish was alarmed by the ignorance and the brutishness they regularly faced, exclaiming, 'we felt we were always pushing shit uphill backwards in Dunedin. There might have been six people in Dunedin who were rooting for us and one of them was our Mum who, incidentally, thought we were mad'.[36] 'We always got the feeling that most people despised us and our music', he continued, 'or liked us and hated the music, or liked the music and hated us. Dunedin bodgies in the late '70s were mean and nasty. Most of my friends back then had been attacked by them'.[37]

Against this backdrop, The Clean continued to cut their teeth by gigging around town, doing the occasional high school dance or playing the halls that dotted the city, as most pubs at the time were reluctant to host young, unknown bands. Robert recalls that when they started to play live, 'there wasn't much of a scene, especially for our kind of stuff. Previously, there had been The Enemy and the first incarnation of The Clean doing the odd gig. It was a case of creating your own gigs and starting a scene, approaching pubs to set up something, often it would be a no'.[38] The indifference of the city's pubs underscored their feeling of being up against it. As Robert notes, getting them on side at the time was a hardscrabble. Along with cover bands, most were still wedded to tried-and-true rock or new wave bands, like The Knobz (a middling power pop band, who, based on the chart success of their independent single, 'Culture?' got a deal with WEA).[39] Publicans were also at ease spoon-feeding the punters classic tunes in the form of countless cover bands that graced the country's pub circuit stages. In contrast, halls like the Old Beneficiaries or Coronation Hall in the suburb of Māori Hill gave bands the freedom to set up shows as they saw fit, where they could bring their own PA, sound person, etc., allowing greater control over the fundamentals (as a few members, and fans, of those bands were under legal drinking age, access to pubs could also be tricky). 'Halls', Robert says, 'were easy to book and put on a show, we would do everything, set up the sound, the door, posters, it was pretty basic but always lots of fun although sometimes the skinheads or boot boys would turn up looking for a fight'.[40] This DIY approach became the default mode in the scene's early days, given the poverty of spaces and resources (including finances). It was an enticing creative solution and fostered a more profound commitment to making music and art on their terms. It was hardening into a deliberate stance that slowly became an ethos, binding the musos and their scene together in a common musical purpose. It was something socially and spatially meaningful. Socially, it stood against those, like the fascist-leaning boot boys (a local variation on skinheads) Robert refers to, spoiling for a fight. Spatially, it meant they avoided being knocked back by pubs and could make the type of sounds they and their audiences wanted to hear.

With greater interest in their live shows and a budding cohort of like-minded bands in town, The Clean and their peers were garnering notice. Some pubs were keen to be involved, most notably The Empire Hotel (often referred to as The Empire

Tavern), which became a strong advocate for the city's musical underground.[41] The Clean was part of a burgeoning scene that confirmed they were on to something good. Robert recalls there was an increase in musical traffic, which was starting to have broader appeal for fans, musos and pubs:

> They were interesting times, people were very keen to come out and see us so we always had a good crowd. There weren't many original bands playing at the start but soon The Same (who turned into The Chills) and Bored Games joined in along with The Verlaines and soon many others. The scene quickly developed, and the pubs realised they could make a bit of money from the gigs, so there were more places to play, and more bands formed, a healthy sense of competition and co-operation was in the air, a very vibrant time.[42]

Big cat

Roy (aka 'Roi') Colbert played a significant role in shaping this burgeoning scene. He ran Dunedin's Records Records (est. 1971) and wrote columns for the local daily *The Evening Star*, the national current events magazine *The Listener* and the music mag *Rip It Up*, among other outlets. He was not unlike Chris Knox, serving as another subcultural custodian and opinionated advocate, but more raconteur to Knox's provocateur. In his many different capacities as an arbiter of taste, Colbert's shop and writing acted as low-level cartography that joined up Dunedin's music scene's mattering and meaning maps. That interplay of texts and contexts provided the crucial advocacy that gave import to what was happening. At the time, in a city where hotels shut at 10.00 pm, shops closed most of the weekend, and where music mags from the UK arrived some three or four months after their publication, people like Colbert were pivotal in rolling out the folklore that would undergird the myth. Colbert was a fount of musical knowledge, a tastemaker who not only advised aspiring musos on the cultural worth of The Incredible String Band or Moby Grape but was a fervent observer and supporter of the city's musical scenes. His reviews and reckonings on international and local acts were an essential part of how those early gigs and initial record releases came into view, framing Dunedin as an unsung musical hotspot not so distant in spirit and sound from what was happening in those cosmopolitan cities a world away.

However, Ōtepoti remained a city captive to its downsides, Colbert reminds readers. Its small-mindedness, he suggests, meant that while what The Clean contributed to the city mattered, a better future lay elsewhere. 'The Clean all realise Dunedin isn't a place to base a rock'n'roll career', he suggests and is 'still considered as welcome as a police raid in the city's hotels … and their numerous local performances have almost all been self-organised'.[43] While a good place to start, any promise of a musical career risked being stunted in Dunedin. David said at the time, the 'best bit was … making the move away and getting recognition somewhere else. Go to Christchurch go to Auckland and suddenly you come back to Dunedin and they say, "oh wow, you're great, you're great" and the pubs start booking you "yeah, you're shit hot", you know. Blah blah blah blah'.[44]

Musing on things later, Colbert saw that getting away from Dunedin, which in his mind didn't know what it was missing, was what The Clean needed to do to step up and become 'proper' musicians. In his estimation, they did. 'They started writing better songs and started learning how to perform them very well', he remarked. 'And all of a sudden they were just an exceptionally good band. They were never really appreciated in Dunedin. They had to go away to Christchurch and to Auckland and then come back to get a proper reaction'.[45]

'Tally Ho!'

Having settled down into the core trio, all writing and singing songs, and with a good number of live sets under their belts, The Clean were eager to get their music on record. There was some interest swirling around them, the keenest coming from a fan based in their northern neighbour up the coast, Ōtautahi/ Christchurch. Roger Shepherd, who worked then at The Record Factory in town, had seen a recent gig at The Gladstone Hotel, which renewed his interest.[46] On a prior trip to Dunedin, he had caught that shaky incarnation of the band playing with The Enemy at one of the Beneficiaries Hall shows. This most recent Ōtautahi concert was a vast improvement, with Robert now firmly in place and the trio playing with proficiency and a cache of new songs. At the time, with North Island outfits well represented by indie labels, through Auckland-based labels like Ripper, Furtive and Propeller or Wellington's Jayrem, and Christchurch and environs brimming with new bands that lacked a presence on record, Shepherd saw an opportunity to capture what was happening down south. The Clean looked to be contenders for his freshly launched label, Flying Nun, and the band was eager to record. Roger thought Propeller or Ripper (at that point distributed by CBS) might snap up The Clean for their first release.[47] Ripper *was* keen on getting the band on board, but the label had its own idea as to which song should be released as a single, a choice that didn't suit the band. Knowing they were currently playing up in Auckland and fearing losing out to another label, Shepherd flew north and asked the band if they'd like to put out a record on Flying Nun. They agreed.

On their way back to Dunedin, the band stopped in Christchurch to record their debut single at Nightshift Studios, helmed by Arnie van Bussell ('studio' is generous; it was run out of the lounge of his flat). At that point, Nightshift was used primarily to record rock and metal bands, and van Bussell didn't know what to do with The Clean. 'A meeting of chalk and cheese' David found it.[48] With lyrics jotted down on a tissue, with the help of Martin Phillipps (The Same/The Chills), on the morning of the session and after five hours in the studio, at a going rate of $10/hr, for a grand total of $50, the band had their first single.[49] Roger recalls, 'it was a totally arbitrary amount, plucked out of thin air, as none of us had any idea how much time or money was involved. The band told Arnie … they had $50 and they wanted to record a song that was it. I guess we got what we paid for'.[50] After half a day in the studio, what they got and paid for was the single 'Tally Ho!'.

'Tally Ho!' is a sharp and snappy piece of garage pop, a rallying cry driven by Robert's exuberant organ riff (played here by Phillipps, credited as Buzz) and hooked to its rousing sing-along chorus. Roy Colbert, reviewing it in *Rip It Up*, finds its shortcomings eclipsed by its DIY gumption:

> "Tally Ho" cost $50 (yep fifty) to make and it sounds a bit that way. If you're looking for mistakes, there are a couple of real boners in there. But it's a great song, it's rock'n'roll heart-pumping hard. And those lusting after that unique Clean sound – thwarted somewhat on the A-side through the inclusion of prominently mixed organ … – have a live

B-side, recorded at the Gladstone by Paul Kean on his trusty
Ferrograph.[51]

As David notes, it's got an unquestionable Question Mark and
the Mysterians verve, a nod to that band's proto-punk single,
'96 Tears'.[52] With its keyboard front and centre and a rough-and-
ready sound, in no small part due to it being recorded on four-
track in an afternoon, back in 1966, 'Tears' shares more than
just a sonic affinity with 'Tally Ho!'. The former was also released
on a small independent label, Pa-Go-Go, and the Mysterians
themselves had to hustle to get it out to radio stations and
record stores, the same DIY attitude driving the band and the
upstart Flying Nun.[53]

However, while it's undoubtedly part of the appeal of 'Tally
Ho!', the far-from-pristine production wasn't in the band's
favour when it came to mainstream radio. 'It's a wonderful
song, but not a single commercial radio station was ever going
to play it, not even once', Shepherd recalls.[54] No commercial
radio play, however, didn't stop 'Tally Ho!' from cracking the Top
20, reaching Number 19, and settling into the charts for seven
weeks. How it wended its way into the charts is revealing. It
did air on student radio, such as it was at the time. Through
that small but soon-to-be important medium, alongside word
of mouth about their live gigs and favourable reviews from
music critics, such as those at *Rip It Up*, enough interest in
the band was built up that retailers and record shops in the
major cities were ordering copies.[55] Slowly, additional stores
picked it up, generating enough sales to get it into the singles
chart (placement on the NZ chart at the time was measured
by sales, not airplay). And through that leg work (literally),
being laid down was a makeshift distribution network, made
up of a few friends of the band and the label, that sat outside

the extant one run by the major labels and handled by their local distributors. In not being aligned with a major label distribution arm, like some of the other independent labels at the time, Flying Nun was steadfast in doing things on its own terms, adopting an informal approach to recording, releasing and distributing that would fit those on its roster very well in these spirited early days.

The chart success of 'Tally Ho!' showed that Flying Nun and the variety of bands it was looking to support might just be able to record and release music as they saw fit. They were entering the realm of the possible. For David, the experience of that single was a lesson learned: 'When we got the test pressing we were disappointed with the sound of it and figured we probably could've made a better job on our 2-track Revox'.[56] Underwhelmed but not undeterred (it was a chart hit, after all), this only encouraged The Clean to get stuck into recording what was to be their follow-up, *Boodle Boodle Boodle*, this time on their terms.

'Tally Ho!' shifted interest in the band, which became decidedly enthusiastic. David recollects that their audience was primarily friends in the late 1970s/early 1980s, but with 'Tally Ho!', The Clean had reached a stage where they could hire halls and put on their own shows. 'This', David recalls, 'is just before the rest of the Dunedin bands popped their heads up and way before anyone talked about a "Dunedin Sound" or even used the word alternative. The general coming together of the scene took a few years until then we felt we were just doing our thing'.[57] Having collaborators committed to creating music differently, 'just doing their thing', orientates that 'doing' away from outside forces that might otherwise threaten or corrupt, such as boot boys and the mainstream music industry and institutions alike. A shared sense of purpose, however inchoate or embryonic, binds music-makers to one another and a place. As David intimates, scenes insulate and incubate, allowing the focusing of creative and social energies around a common interest, in this case making music, orientated away from those forces that might otherwise work against it. That commonality is nurtured in shared spaces, through venues, rehearsal spaces, record shops, flats, etc., by media interest, such as *Rip It Up*, *In Touch*, *Otago Daily Times*, student radio, and an enthusiastic label in the budding Flying Nun. Aligned as such, they affirm a feeling of solidarity, of being in it (and against it) together. In turn, this shapes an alternative ethos at a time, as David notes, well before that adjective became a cynically generic marketing term. As others join in, another world of possibility comes into view: an ability to imagine new sorts of cultural spaces becomes increasingly plausible, doable even. And in those early days, 'doable' still meant doing-it-yourself with like-minded collaborators. In this 'doing', something exceptional could materialize. The success of 'Tally Ho!' confirmed this and was a welcome boost for the label. But it was *Boodle* that sinched it.

2 *Boodle Boodle Boodle*

With Boodle we wanted to make interesting recordings, not just record the band as we were live and then embellish that. We knew a lot of our fave music was recorded on a two-track tape machine, four tracks, etc., so we knew it was possible to make very good recordings on limited equipment. There's a misconception sometimes that we were lo-fi fans but the opposite was the case from the get go really. **– DAVID KILGOUR**[1]

While on tour plugging 'Tally Ho!', The Clean briefly holed up in Auckland in early September of 1981. By now, the band's DIY musical chops had been well-honed, making the most of working with less. This included booking their own tours of halls and pubs, using their own PA, driving themselves from gig to gig up and down the country, and putting down lots of demos on their Revox B77 2-track recorder. All of this served them well when it came to recording the EP. David recalls he and Hamish already had 'Anything Could Happen' and 'Point That Thing' well and truly sorted before Robert joined, and with further rehearsing, jamming and co-writing, they were primed to get things down on tape. '(We) had also toured NZ twice before doing *Boodle* along with many Dunedin shows. After recording ourselves on a 2-track Revox and then Chris Knox buying his 4-track, we saw we could make a good recording with Doug Hood and Chris. We kinda taught ourselves how to play while writing songs and then taught ourselves how to record and overdub'.[2]

David saw in the *Boodle* session an opportunity to play with the act of recording itself, to get some of that liveness down on tape and to experiment with the technology and test its limits. He notes that the experience and recorded result of 'Tally Ho!' was 'a big letdown, so again we were learning as we went'.[3] Now more confident and tauter, a new record would ideally showcase the band's quintessence. Armed only with a four-track recorder, they could try out some new approaches to getting it right here. The constraints required a bit of creative dexterity, which meant there wasn't much faffing about with overdubs and multiple tracks. Roger recalls some of the decision-making around the tech and the format:

> They just thought they could record The Clean better on Chris's 4-track than we could otherwise. The feeling was that there's five or six songs ready to record; let's just go with that and make an EP. It takes out the stress of trying to put an album together. That was the great thing about the EP format: a lot of the bands that came after them had an EP's worth of songs but not an album's worth, and it reduced the whole stress of recording.[4]

The EP format suited everyone as it allowed more exploration over a greater number of songs and the kind of economy dictated by the four-track. This being settled, it was time to commit things to tape.

Secret place

The recording space they had in mind in Auckland was a tiny, ramshackle place: The Legion of Frontiersmen Hall, which doubled as a Scout Hall, on Bond Street, near the inner-city suburb of Grey Lynn. Over a couple of days, The Clean thrashed out the selection of songs on a four-track that would become the *Boodle* EP. With most of these already well-rehearsed through countless gigs, the trick in such a small space was figuring out how to get everything mixed down to four tracks and how best to make the sound of the room work for the songs. That meant getting the tech in place as best as possible. Robert shares some of the details of working in such a small space:

> We set up our amps in the main hall, roughly 6x6 metres. The 4-track and mixing desk were in a little side room. We set up as though in the practice room all facing each other, there was no sound separation so amps and drums were close-miked, although there were some room mikes, too. There was a guide vocal recorded, and maybe once this was the final vocal, but I would be surprised. We would pretty much get a good take within one or two goes from memory. Once we had the five songs done it was a case of what do they need overdub wise, usually extra guitars and a main vocal, backing vocals and sometimes percussion.[5]

He continues:

> It was a case of choosing which ones to do …. Recording wise, there were only four tracks to use so we had to plan it carefully, for example, what instruments were going on which tracks, from memory it was bass, guitar and drums on two tracks to give a good spread of sound and with this it was all about getting a good live sound as there was no separation in the room, and of course getting a good signal through the mikes onto the desk. Doug Hood was great at this as he had done a lot of live sound and engineering, he was a natural. The other two tracks were taken up with vocals

and any other overdubs, mostly second guitars. It did vary a little from song to song, so sometimes we would have a guitar and a vocal being done at the same time and bounced down to the track. It was all very quick, natural and easy. Everything sounded good as it went down so there was no need to second guess or change the way we did things.[6]

Regarding how the creative labour was divided up, Doug, who, with The Enemy, Toy Love and others, had plenty of live mixing under his belt, tended to the sound engineering. He brought some valuable ideas about gear placement around the room. Chris was the ideas person, though he could chip in with some tech help 'if that means things like mic placement and equalization, etc., both very encouraging, constructively critical'. Bob Sutton, a friend of Doug's, hovered around the recording session, helping with gear and chipping in with the odd lyrical and production ideas.[7] Ultimately, it worked because they all 'shared similar musical tastes and similar ideas on how to record and what our basic goals were'.[8] Good friends committed to recording five songs on four tracks with three band members over two days to get one EP: *Boodle Boodle Boodle*.

'Billy Two'

Given that violence formed the backdrop against which the band had struggled to define themselves in Ōtepoti, 'Billy Two' is a brusque starter for the EP. It's a skittish, frantic homage to a bully 'who never ever spoke'. Having punched David in the face at a local pool hall, Billy, the song's taciturn antagonist, is centre stage in a slice of Dunedin realism that serves as the EP's opening scene. Inspired partly by The Kinks, it's also a nod to 'British power pop style (that we were all into), and it always went down well live', Robert recalls.[9] Hamish's drums punctuate David's brisk flurry of acoustic strums that launch the song, and Robert's sturdy bass kicks in. The lyrics sketch the scene of confrontation, courage plucked up to meet again, and the bully is left speechless. The middle eight is bridged with a judicious stretch of backwards masking. It's a clever, disorienting psychedelic touch, complete with a drum-fill skirmish from Hamish. Then the song's playful freneticism triumphantly kicks back into gear through to its finish until 'I guess that's all gone', done and dusted. It's a raucous pop song of nervy assuredness that sets the tenor for the rest of the EP.

'Thumbs Off'

'Thumbs Off' gives us Robert's first lyrics and lead vocals on a Clean record, a song he describes as 'instant driving pop'.[10] He said at the time of its release that it refers to a friend, adding to the *Boodle* entourage, who was going through a harrowing housing situation, out of pocket, on the street and friendless.[11] With our lead character bereft, unstable and alone, it has a malaise that belies its pop-song impulses, with Robert lamenting, 'sometimes I just feel too much, and I don't want to feel at all'. David adds some adroitly paced guitar strokes to daub the verses, striding towards the chorus, where he launches into that searing guitar sound. Here, it sounds hemmed in, pushing the absolute limits of what the magnetic tape could bear. The noise is tamped down; it's less buzzsaw and more beeline. A coarse melodic backdrop, it props up the chorus's quizzical 'who's gonna pay the bills today, who's gonna turn the girls away … and who's gonna make you feel okay'. It's the song that comes under the most self-criticism, somewhat unfairly. Hamish described it as a 'little flat'.[12] For David, it 'wasn't as good as the version on Odditties. Not as bouncy, beaty meat'.[13] Roger Shepherd finds it 'a bit plodding', but 'a welcome contrast to the other material and has historical importance as the recorded debut of Robert's unique and world-famous seemingly off-key singing style'.[14] He echoes Scott's assessment of his singing as being a 'bit crap'.[15] All of these add to its jaunty, muddle-headed charm, and it was a live favourite, too.

'Anything Could Happen'

The last song on Side One opens with a fulsome acoustic guitar strum that sets up a low-slung, twangy electric guitar line, joined by Robert's limber bass, with Hamish marching us in on drums. As Robert hears it, that combination gives it a 'country rock swing, a nice mix of electric and acoustic guitar'.[16] Hamish, looking back at it in early 2012, remembered they were going for a 'Highway 61/Rolling Stones country feel' born from a great affection for '20th Century folk, blues and country'.[17] David's frank about the joy of a new skill set, 'at the stage of my guitar playing where I'm excited just to play a barre chord, let alone put a chord progression together. Really!'.[18] This shines through in the song's upbeat melodies, even though the lyrics paint a downbeat picture. It's another slice-of-life bit of realism, this time coming from Hamish:

> It was funny cos a current girlfriend was discovered by me on my visit working in this same company for this asshole and she hated the job intensely. She was a trained graphic artist. He's the doctor who points me to a junkyard – that's my

Dylan reference – and she's my junkyard angel. The whole song is a nod to Bob, with the imagery of empty doorways and highways.[19]

In his characteristic reflective fashion, Hamish sees it as a 'pretty simple song'.[20] It does, however, have some personal and social import, very much indebted to a way of life in New Zealand, Dunedin in particular. Musing about it thirty years later, Hamish extols its social critique and the title's contrasting invocation of hopefulness:

> I think my reading of Kerouac and Ginsberg and Burroughs informed the optimistic, Buddhistic chorus with the verses essentially being negative, echoing confusing social messages and behaviour, hypocrisy and the ridiculous weight given to so called authority. Alienation and despair. We were reacting to our parents' conservative ideology and mindset and conservative New Zealand culture.[21]

Out of this comes a catchy riff on folk-pop with a healthy, relaxed beatnik vibe and the added intrigue of its peculiar cast of characters. All of this gels around its choral counsel: 'The choice is yours, so make it worthwhile', a sentiment that nimbly sums up The Clean's sensibility, *Boodle*, and its historical moment.

'Sad Eyed Lady'

'Sad Eyed Lady' kicks off Side Two, introducing us to another character in the *Boodle* retinue: a smiling, enigmatic figure sitting at the edge of town. David, who threw the song together in 'five minutes', describes it as 'trying to imitate Syd

Barret, solo'. 'I wrote it as a pisstake of [him] one day by turning on the Revox and writing the song straight off'.[22] There is a hint of Barrett's obtuse psychedelic folksiness coming through, like that heard on 'No Good Trying' or 'Octopus' from *The Madcap Laughs* (1970). In a titular nod to Dylan's 'Sad-Eyed Lady of the Lowlands' (1966), it differs from the waltz-time of its namesake by following its own offbeat time signature, what Robert calls 'angular skewed pop with great changes'.[23] Time is the villain in this scenario, beginning with the faint counting in '1 2 3 4', edging into its beguiling slackness. This settles into an off-kilter lilt full of reverb, which is pared down to give more space to the guitar, occasionally off-key vocals and drums, all valiantly slogging on. The resulting echo, the vocal drawl lingering over the lyrics and the ringing guitars all play up the sound of the dilapidated Scout Hall, pushing out the song's edges to create a cavernous, affectless void where everything and everyone is left hanging. The monotony of this barren tableau is meted out through its sobering time checks of 'one o'clock' and 'two o'clock' (counted out by Hamish's snare). Chris Knox is heard wailing behind the repeated refrain 'it's time to go', a languid incantation that sees out the song's second half and only adds to its world weariness. Graeme Downes noted that, at the time, a 'bunch of Clean fans painted the lyrics on the outside of their Clyde street flat such that it was colloquially known as the "Time to Go" house for the best part of a decade'.[24]

'Point That Thing Somewhere Else'

As the sparest track on the EP, 'Sad Eyed Lady' is a disarming starter for Side Two, a droll palate-cleanser making way for the undulating majesty of 'Point That Thing Somewhere Else'.

Another well-loved live favourite and the longest track on *Boodle*, clocking in at over 5 minutes and occupying a third of the EP's playing time. It opens with a quick flourish, a descending gyre of sounds with the band searching for someplace to pitch up for what's about to unfold. They lock onto Hamish's motorik drumming, which pounds out the four-four beat, never deviating and always true. David's guitar sounds veer between scorching the stratosphere and plumbing the depths of the Kermadec Trench, plying out intertwining laminae of distortion. Robert's bass cuts through the ensuing roar, carving out the song's central furrow while Hamish intones coolly about a failing relationship. It has a feel of menace running counterpoint to its resoluteness, with layered guitar riffs contorting around the bass and drums, which hold the line. Hamish deadpans 'up and down to the speed freak sound', obtuse lyrics just breaching the surface of a turbid sea of white noise yoked to the song's driving rhythm section. It sounds as though they're channelling the Velvet Underground's monument to feedback, 'European Son' (which closes their eponymous debut LP), as if harnessed to the surf groove of Dick Dale. Without a doubt, though, this is very much their own thing, *their* speed freak sound.

The song preceded this incarnation of the band, with its bassline written by Peter Gutteridge in the first iteration of The Clean. He recalls the power of the music and how it, and the band, gelled as it came about:

> David and Hamish are just such good players. David & I just work together well, we seem to mesh. I know the way he plays. When we wrote 'Point That Thing' we didn't have any understanding at all, it just sounded good. It was the simplest thing. I had this really raw sort of distorting bass stack & this

really light bass sound that sounded like a guitar bass. It was just one of those things you start playing & 'hey, that sounds good' & you could play it for a long time. You don't spend ages writing a song like that, it just comes. Hamish put some words to it & it was written the next day.[25]

That fortuitous moment of things falling into place through a jam, without overthinking it, gives 'Point' much of its mesmeric thrum. Gutteridge refers to his bass line as a God chord, a fullness that came out at the live gigs.[26] David recalls putting it on tape gave it a different sound and shape. As one of their earliest songs, it was a regular part of their set for a few years by the time they came to record it, and it had a distinctive energy and feel that became something else when recorded and stood out in the session. 'Recording "Point That Thing" seemed very special straight away. Up until this point we had been playing it quite fast but for the recording we pulled back a bit', Robert notes. For him, it stands out still, all 'Eastern swirling guitar drones'. At the *Boodle* session, he felt it came down to 'capturing a good version … it was different every time we played it'.[27]

After reflecting on it decades later, David remains fond of the mysterious aspect of the song and is still vexed by it. 'I don't know what it is about that song', he says. 'It was a bit of a pivotal moment coming up with that track', he continues, 'up until that point, we had been playing it as quite a metallic fast track. I think by the time we came to record it, we were a bit tired of that and we just went the opposite way. I think once we had done the guitar overdub, we knew we were onto something pretty special'.[28] The recorded version could have been different, 'better in so many ways, but it was good we did it so simply as it could have been ruined. A slightly more metal version would have been good though!!'.[29]

'Point That Thing' does evoke that tone of paranoia that Hamish once suggested courses through The Clean's early period ('Don't point me out in the crowd/Don't point that thing at me'), not entirely misplaced given when and where the song and EP came together. However, this contrasts with its ineluctable propulsion, a sense of determination and uplift that powers through, lending it a solidity that elevates it to the monumental. The song is a perfect capstone, a tour-de-force finale for a kaleidoscopic five-song suite of textures and tales. *Boodle* is a miniature masterpiece of scenic sequencing, opening with the up-close-and-personal violence of a pool-hall punch-up and closing with a glimpse of the sublime effortlessly wrought out of the musical clamour. The occasional allusions to ennui and uncertainty, a catalogue of the thoughts and feelings of the lost, lonely and wayward, the beaten up and the beaten down, with its wry observations and ethnography of the motley crew that populates its songs – eccentrics and exes, doctors, dancers and dullards, friends and enemies – the darker inclinations of *Boodle* are buoyed by flashes of enlivening optimism. There's a brio here, a salubrious DIY flair set on pushing out the limits of what's possible, musically and technically. It bears an irrepressible trace of the fervid amateurism of 'Tally Ho!', but now they're a band more in control, of both their sound and how best to render it. There's also a dialectical gist to the EP that still resonates: a dynamism born of trial and error, playing the taut off the loose, a knowingness pitted against the unknown, hope against despair, all invigorating tensions that showcase a band setting out onto new musical terrain. It pulses throughout *Boodle*, animating an eclectic alloy of sharp melodic detailing poking through hazy swathes of white noise and spacey reverb, twinned motifs fastened together in a cannily balanced tranche of post-punk pop-rock.

All those notes

That everything fell into place quickly and easily wasn't a surprise to anyone involved. The Clean, Hood says, was 'a wonderfully great live band' by then, so 'most of those songs were done in one or two takes'.[30] In recalling the constraints, Hood was chuffed with what they got on tape. It was 'incredibly exciting. You never really knew at the end of the take whether you had a good recording'.[31] Robert also remembers hearing it for the first time, fresh after their recording session ended:

> We would have done a quick mix at the end of the session but I can't remember doing the main mix. Chris was free with his opinions on what should happen with the songs, we took his ideas on board, but really we knew what we wanted it to sound like, the finished article didn't change much at all from the quick mixes we did at the end of tracking. I do remember being amazed listening back to how exciting and vibrant it sounded, we knew we had created something special.[32]

This was the consummate result for a band that wanted to have as much oversight as possible over their sound.

> The recording process was very cheap and we had total control. Doug worked out how to mic us up and get it all down to four tracks. Mixing four tracks, especially if recorded well, is very easy and very quick. We mixed the drums and bass to one track usually, having three more tracks for more bouncing or guitars, vocals, etc.[33]

Still, Knox thought it awful and insisted they head to Mandrill Studios, in nearby Parnell, and let a proper studio engineer have a go.

For the modest sum of $750, the session defined 'cheap and cheerful'. Working with time, tech and financial constraints drew on all their DIY nous, well-honed by then. The five friends made a record the way they wanted, overseeing and controlling nearly everything. They even followed the tapes down to the EMI pressing plant in Wellington to ensure the record pressers didn't flatten the sound out (for which they were notorious). It's an all-in collaboration born of a shrewd craftiness resulting in the shared triumph of doing it their own way. In short order, it would become a defining musical moment.

Alongside the clutch of *Boodle* songs, what The Clean, Hood, and Knox had also laid down in the session was an approach to recording that became a preferred mode of production for several of Flying Nun's subsequent releases. Knox had been experimenting with the TEAC four-track solo and in tandem with his former Enemy and Toy Love bandmate Alec Bathgate in their new duo, The Tall Dwarfs. These initial recordings, and the debut album by Auckland outfit Techtones, *TT 23* (Ripper, 1981), recorded on the four-track with Hood and Knox, convinced The Clean this was the way to go for *Boodle*. Knox was deeply enamoured with this approach, not least for what it did for realizing creative potential but also for doing it your way, without the hassle of know-it-alls who had in their mind how a song should properly sound. 'The freedom was amazing', he says, 'not having some stupid engineer who had never heard your cruddy music saying "you can't do that, you can't do that, you can't do that" and foisting their own idea of what a good record sounded like upon you was just like "Yes. Yes. Just give us more of this"'.[34] Knox noted his preference for the limitations four tracks imposed because 'you can get better sound with limited tracks', but also the distinctive texture it gives a recording. 'It's little chunks of metal oxide hurtling around on a piece of cellulose, which gives rougher edges', he enthuses, 'you've got these irregular blobs of metal that interact together, give a little shock of electricity that registers as sound and it's just bloody magic'.[35] That gave *Boodle* (and many of those early Flying Nun records) its distinctive graininess, what for better or worse many would later call 'lo-fi'.

The notion of 'lo-fi' soon got attached to The Clean and others in the Flying Nun stable. This likely emerged due to the quick recording sessions, rapid-release turnarounds and the pace at which Doug and Chris chose to work. Things were pushed to their limits, with little time or need for fuss or muss. However, contrary to the fascination for what became known elsewhere as 'lo-fi', here it's more of a misnomer.[36] There was something that approached a sonic clarity in early Flying Nun records like *Boodle*, a greater sense of allegiance to the fidelity of the performance gained by capturing a 'liveness', those perfect imperfections, in the recording moment. With Knox very much in mind, Bruce Russell (of Dunedin's noisy improv band The Dead C, an early employee of Flying Nun and later founder of Xpressway Records) refers to this mode of production as 'mis-competence', a non-standard use of technology as an improvised response to the various constraints faced by music-makers in Aotearoa. Beginning with Douglas Lilburn, an early, local exemplar of electronic composition, he situates such an approach to recording within a historical continuum, bound up in the nexus of technology, musical composition and myth in New Zealand. The response manifests as a sensibility, Russell asserts, 'related directly to not only the Antipodean DIY myth – a romantic conception of New Zealanders as uniquely possessing ingenuity and resourcefulness, able to make do with whatever scrap materials are at hand – but also the punk ethos of "just doing it" and "sticking it to the man"'.[37] Knox acknowledges much the same in reflecting on *Boodle*:

> People were quite surprised by the results, particularly Doug, who managed to squeeze out of this damn thing. When he was involved in the recording we were going through a desk, a live sound desk. It was for live mixing, it wasn't a beautiful studio desk by any matter of means … You had to capture the performance, to a great degree, rather than going in and fixing things in the mix and doing heaps of overdubs. It just wasn't that sort of recording. So there's a life to those early Flying Nun things that was really valuable. And I think that's what a lot of people overseas heard … I think in New Zealand a lot of people were inspired too that you could get in the Top 10 on something that was recorded for bugger all on anti-diluvian equipment but accessible equipment. I think it just makes things more accessible for those who had no chance of getting on big labels because big labels weren't interested at the time anyway.[38]

Listening to it nearly forty years later, David still marvels at what they pulled off: 'I heard those tracks straight off tape recently for the first time in quite a long time and I was really surprised at how good they sounded. Especially the drums and bass, which were coming off one track'.[39] As Kilgour's astonishment attests, and Russell suggests, the power, what Knox calls here the 'life', ascribed to this particular mode of production and the role the TEAC four-track played in *Boodle* and future recordings added a gritty foundational substrate to the myth. It further cemented the links between DIY, as an ethos of practicality, creative control and democratic collaboration built from the ground up, and the adaptation of technology as a home-spun assemblage of whatever bits and bobs are available. Wedding agency to necessity, it made a local virtue out of the ad hoc and bespoke. Responding to distance and accessibility resulted in the compelling merger of the material and symbolic through music-making in Aotearoa, in which The Clean and their peers were actively engaged (soon to be held up as icons). In their case, it took hold as a sensibility that would shortly coalesce into a signature sound.

Pop art pictures

Visuals were essential to the band and Flying Nun, becoming another defining characteristic of The Clean and the label's aesthetic. Robert notes the band members were artists beyond their musical talents, 'very interested in the visual world and the use of image, we always had ideas floating around and we always did our own posters'.[40] Each band member had come up with a drawing for the cover. 'No one could choose or decide', he recalls, and, in the end, as the EP credits quip, 'bloody Chris Knox again' won out (the members' attempts at cover images appear on the backside of the EP).[41] Knox based his black-and-white sketch on a photo by Carol Tippet, where the band is crammed into a bathtub, fully clothed but soaking wet, snapped during a photo shoot for the EP. 'I'm not sure who first came up with the idea of using the bath for The Clean photo shoot', she says, continuing, 'I've always just assumed it was probably a play on the band name'. She recalls that Chris was filming it, and Doug looked after the lighting. There was 'a sense of the absurdity of it all, which was key to creating a memorable image'.[42] Tippet was actively photographing this new cohort of outfits populating music scenes across the country, providing images for album and band promos, and regularly doing shoots for magazines, particularly *Rip It Up* (she flatted then with Barbara Ward and Knox, who were a couple, and Hood, which allowed a 'relaxed familiarity' to settle in for the shoot).[43] She was an essential documenter of scenes and bands across the country throughout Aotearoa, and her images are core to the visual culture binding this emergent new musical world together. Several of Carol's photos are iconic, forming part of the visual lexicon of what became the 'Dunedin Sound' and offering a pictorial testament to an alternate musical world unfolding across the country.

Initial pressings of the EP came with a sixteen-page comic, which was Knox's idea again. All the band members, including Chris, were budding artists and contributed to the comic, as did their friends, Martin Phillipps, Ian Dalziel, Jenny Halliday and others. Various doodles extoll the virtues of The Clean ('The Clean do not sing about religion … The Clean do not sing about sex … The Clean do sing about animals … The Clean do not necessarily rhyme'), while others took on the mainstream music industry. Dalziel, for example, recently returned to New Zealand after doing live sound for Toy Love during their stint in Australia, sketched out a 'Quick Quiz' ('7 correct answers means you are now ready for success and all the trappings … go directly to Australia/Do not collect $200'). David finds the comic 'quite cryptic really', which might also have to do with the pagination being mixed up during printing.[44] Early promotional copies of *Boodle* came with a pop-up cut-out of the band, with several glowing reviews of The Clean, another Knox idea (both this and the comic are the bonus touches that would later up the resale value for first pressings among overseas record collectors).[45] This attention to detail, craftsmanship and collaboration became a hallmark of Flying Nun records.

Boodle Boodle Boodle, the curiously offbeat title for the EP, was settled upon after a suggestion from Barbara Ward, Chris's partner. And that, too, is something cryptic. The word has different meanings. It's a euphemistic curse word that Ward's family used and also refers to money, usually of the ill-gotten variety and a joking reference to how much the band might earn from it (you could be forgiven then for hearing in its title a sly sing-songy nod to ABBA's 'Money Money Money'). Given the sum and substance of the EP, both are on point.

The cover and title sorted and the comic inserted, the first pressing of *Boodle* was ready to go, to be released in early November 1981. Everyone involved was chuffed with how it all came together, and they knew they had something special. But how *Boodle* would fare once released into the wild was anybody's guess.

3 Aftermath

I think one of the most important things is getting our own musical identity – getting rid of our colonial mentality. Other New Zealand art forms like our films have been accepted overseas. There's no reason why our records shouldn't. — **HAMISH KILGOUR**[1]

With *Boodle*, The Clean signalled they had arrived, bearing a message that something *sui generis* was stirring down south. Weighing in on it at the time, Roy Colbert was gobsmacked, claiming it was 'almost disbelievingly well-recorded … this is more than even us fans hoped for. "Tally Ho!" was for the already-converted: *Boodle* is for everyone'.[2] It entered the Top 50 singles chart, slotting in at Number 5, and stayed on the charts for six months. During that run, it rubbed shoulders with hits from overseas artists like Anne Murray, Phil Collins, John Lennon, ELO, Juice Newton, Loverboy, Kool and the Gang and Stars on 45, among a smattering of local releases. By the end of 1982, it was the nation's best-selling domestic single. Like 'Tally Ho!', it reached its rank as a chart hit without airplay on commercial radio, another ornery musical oddity from the band that ratcheted up both their and the EP's mythical status.

That mainstream radio ignored it wasn't such a surprise. Commercial stations and the state broadcaster, Radio New Zealand, wanted polish. This was anathema to the band. 'We weren't an easy sell', David says, 'nasty treble, out of tune vocals, tough attitude, etcetera, but I think the music really did speak for itself'.[3] Instead, the record shops, student radio, video shows, such as *Radio with Pictures*, music mags like *Rip It Up* and

In Touch, write-ups in the local press and the constant touring gave the band and the EP the necessary traction. It was a multi-pronged, grassroots approach that defied the orthodoxy and worked a charm. Roger Shepherd was triumphant:

> It showed all those bands what could be done on a 4-track and it eased a lot of bands that would've been freaked out in a studio environment by the expense and the snooty attitude of the people that worked in them. A lot of those bands would've reacted really badly to that. It also showed them what the sales potential was … I thought it was good enough to do really well, but it was top five in the charts twice. It was up there before Christmas and then bounced back up after Christmas, so it gives you an idea of just how much interest there was in it and how much people liked it. It sold on a grassroots level of people seeing the band, or people talking about it in record shops or people reading music writers in newspapers and *Rip It Up*. Commercial radio never played it, so it was a bit of an 'up yours' gesture, the whole thing.[4]

The distribution network Shepherd set up for Flying Nun, cobbled together out of personal connections, circumvented the major label network. This needs to be seen alongside other industries and institutions that were sympathetic to what the label and bands were doing. If independent music-making in Aotearoa was to have real legs, it needed to work in concert with like-minded entities. This meant a dalliance with local media and musical institutions. Though the landscape was changing, identifying allies from a thin slate of options still took some effort. In an early Flying Nun newsletter, Hamish asked, 'Why didn't the bloody radio stations play *Boodle*? (The $1000 question).'[5] Shepherd is candid about what that meant for artists on the label and that commercial success should not be the end goal. 'Being on Flying Nun was probably a hindrance for a band when it came to commercial radio', he says, recalling that 'they hated us, with the perception being that everything we did was poorly recorded and rather strange'.[6] To that end, the label 'always worked closely with the student stations', which was a disjointed patchwork at this stage. More would eventually come online and align to form a stable national network. 'They were the only radio outlets for most of our releases and their listeners tended to be our bands' core audience'.[7]

The state of airwaves in the country at the time of *Boodle* was a mix of private/commercial, public broadcasting, community and an evolving student radio network, all of which had differing interests and remits. Private/commercial radio was well-ensconced by the end of the 1970s. The most prominent was Radio Hauraki, the country's legendary pirate radio station, which began its broadcasting career offshore of Auckland in 1966. Initially modelling itself after the UK's pirate pioneer Radio Caroline, it was granted a commercial licence and became landlocked in 1970. This move impacted what was heard on the airwaves, meaning more rock and pop. In 1981, the national public broadcaster, RNZ, was still very much beholden to a BBC-like programming model, which had as its remit the education and edification of its audience. While there was a place for music in their programming, pop and rock were low priorities, which could be better left with the commercial stations to plug. Student radio was in its infancy nationwide but was gaining a profile. In Dunedin, it was patchy, with an annual broadcast airing on 4XT (aka Radio Ripper) during Orientation Week, the yearly ritual whereby new students are initiated into university life (and where many independent bands would play, including The Clean and other Flying Nun acts). Those initial short-term blasts, before 1984, were a peculiarity of New Zealand broadcasting authorizations, temporary warrants that allowed student radio to establish itself. This was a 'distinctive innovation' unique to the country, carving out a space between commercial radio and public broadcasters within which they started to thrive.[8] While initially they would be expected to cater to a university audience, airing news and promoting student-relevant events, they began to play more music, with a pronounced youth focus and drawing from new releases in Aotearoa, particularly what the independent labels were putting out. Licences until the 1980s were only granted for intermittent transmission, typically finishing at the end of the university year as students left campus. Of this idiosyncratic broadcasting rhythm, Roger Shepherd noted that (in 1982) 'sales of our records plummet when student radio goes off the air'.[9]

Another key promotional avenue was music programmes on TV, a conduit that allowed the underground to encroach into mainstream New Zealand via their living rooms stealthily. As is the case elsewhere, historically these have been essential platforms for promoting popular music from international and local artists. Almost from its inception in 1960, local television, then a single channel run by NZBC, had devoted timeslots to music. Most often, these consisted of mimed clips on shows such as *Into the Groove* (1962–4) and *C'mon* (1966–9), the latter of which was a knock-off of its American counterparts like *Hullaballoo*, complete with go-go girls. Mostly, they were content with airing NZ-based covers of international hits, following a standard hit parade format, but the odd local original found its way into the programming. In the mid-1970s, around the time of the dissolution of the NZBC into Radio New

Zealand and two TV channels, Television One and Television Two (the latter would briefly be renamed South Pacific Television), a quaintly anarchic pop-culture programme with a musical bent, *Grunt Machine*, aired for a year on TV One.[10] Around the same time, two new music video showcases with greater longevity appeared on TV Two/SPT: *Ready to Roll* (*RTR*), running from 1975–2001, and *Radio with Pictures* (*RWP*), aired from 1976 to 1989.[11] *RTR* played straighter fare, while *RWP* quickly adopted a leftfield position, taking advantage of overseas punk and new wave as it began to bloom. This came primarily through one of its first on-air hosts, Barry Jenkin (also known as Dr. Rock), who helmed a show on Radio Hauraki.

Jenkin was a critical musical gatekeeper, not just for the Hauraki connections but also for his access to music that would not otherwise find its way into New Zealand shops due to local import restrictions. These were placed on record manufacturing and distribution in the country then. EMI dominated the local market, overseeing manufacture and distribution, and most international releases were pressed in-country. Owing to New Zealand's modest population, this typically meant that proven overseas hits got the go-ahead for local pressing and national release. Import restrictions ensured this, cementing the major labels' stranglehold on the music scene. However, local labels did a reasonable job of getting some New Zealand pop and rock artists into the mix, but of the more agreeable sort. For a genre like punk, however, with little hope of promotion through radio airplay on most of the nation's radio stations, it was much harder to come by. As Lee Borrie notes, 'for punk fans eager to import records into New Zealand, individuals were restricted to expenditure of just $100 per annum (including postage), and import licenses were rare for retailers, meaning university bookshops were among the few to stock imported records'. Hauraki had an exemption to the import restrictions, granting Jenkin a point of entry into this new musical world. He could play music many fans could not yet buy locally, putting him at the vanguard. Jenkin was also getting video clips from many overseas punk and new wave bands, and the labels were sending them along as bonus promotional odds and ends. *RWP* quickly became the platform to plug these new sights and sounds.

With such a rarefied promotional arsenal, while being left to their own devices by the higher-ups at TV2, *RWP* adopted a clever programming tactic: inserting videos from local artists between international clips. Brett Hansen (producer for *RWP*) saw this as 'a public service'. 'We took it really seriously and there was so much debate', he recalls, and they 'worked long hours trying to get things together for it, even though sometimes it looked a bit amateurish at times. We saw this as a channel of record. Not only for our local music but primarily to make local music work – [and] to have it sit in parallel to what was happening contemporarily'.[12] At the end of the decade, this meant acts like Toy Love and some other bands had their music seen and heard when commercial radio refused them airplay. This was essential to reaching a broader audience in ways that touring could not, and commercial radio refused to, making *RWP* a unique promotional platform.

Karyn Hay took over the presenter role in 1981, coming on board with a solid pedigree as the first female rock DJ on Radio Hauraki. Her arrival was timely, as the independent music scene was taking hold, and the availability of videos from Flying Nun artists (alongside other independent acts) was increasing. Added to this was Hay's New Zealand accent, which had not been bent into broadcast-standard English (often referred to as 'British English' or 'BBC pronunciation'), having avoided the elocution lessons that were otherwise prescribed for TV presenters. This set her apart from her colleagues and added to the nascent New Zealand-ness that reinforced the show's local flavour, as seen and heard in the surge of home-grown indie videos. *RWP* had now settled into its Sunday night slot, airing before the regularly scheduled horror movie. Hitting a demographic sweet spot, it was appointment viewing. For many people making independent music, this was the time and place to hear and see what they and their peers were up to. Given the state of commercial radio at the time, this was a critical medium, as you heard local music and saw it, adding to its distinctive visual lexicon and lending better definition, invoking Raymond Williams, to an emergent structure of feeling.

Many Flying Nun bands entered the nation's living rooms through *RWP*. The Clean were no exception. The clip for 'Tally Ho!', shot by Chris Knox up in Auckland, is a pixelated ode to the filmmakers Norman McLaren and local Len Lye (both known for their scratching experiments through manipulating film stock to create abstract animation).[13] Its stop-motion style fits well with the song's chirpy freneticism. 'Anything Could Happen' was chosen to plug *Boodle,* and the promo video took a similarly humorous turn. Shot in Christchurch, it features the trio playing at various sites around the city, including its famous Cathedral Square (not far from Flying Nun HQ) and, taking the lyrics literally, a junkyard. Andrew Shaw, who was working for TVNZ then, directed the clip. 'The first time I heard it, I was captivated', he says. 'We decided to shoot it near the arts centre and a rubbish tip and tried to remain true to the lyrics. Cue an old wheel quietly rolling into frame'[14]. As was the case with many of the promotional clips for up-and-coming New Zealand bands, it was shot on the short-ends of a film reel, those remaindered bits that hadn't been used up for a proper TVNZ news story ('and some of it stolen', Shaw recalls).[15] These quintessentially DIY efforts were often meant to be aired only once to plug a new band's single or album, so rarely was there much thought put into things like *mise en scène*, though occasionally a hint of experimentation and style crept in, as was the case with 'Anything'. What many of these clips had in common was putting the band or artist at the centre, allowing fans to put faces and figures to the voices they heard on the record.

Gem

Boodle was a definitive turning point for the band. 'For whatever reason, it seemed to grab people's attention', Robert recalls, 'it stood out at the time as being different, bright and fresh'.[16] For David, its impact was evident at once, with larger crowds at the gigs, increased sales, etc., all of which came with some satisfaction, not only for the effort they had been putting in since those early days but also confirmed their approach to making music was the right one. 'Hamish and I had been working towards this for two years or longer if you go back to the bedroom', he says, and 'that we did it via the DIY ethic was gratifying and gave us momentum'. Thinking back, David knew 'we had made a mark but on our own terms. We did notice the reaction from the music establishment, surprise and horror combined, which again gave us more energy to stick it to the man'.[17]

'Sticking it to the man' was how The Clean, their peers and Flying Nun set about doing things, an animating principle that governed those early days. This was how the band would approach the industry throughout its career. From the word go, it kept the group at arm's length, simply ignoring them. This was contrary to how other media, such as *Rip It Up*, *In Touch*, student radio and *RWP*, were otherwise embracing the band. 'The reviews were all very good. It enabled Flying Nun and ourselves to move forward in the ways we wanted. A cornerstone, a building block', Robert recollects.[18] For The Clean, it was an affirmation that allowed them to carry on as they saw fit. For Flying Nun, that building block came in the form of some financial grounding, and the label's movement forward would be an exhilarating, if not always easy, one. All up, it was, as Robert suggests, 'a pivotal moment for NZ music in some eyes'.[19]

Band that never was

In 1982, not long after the release of *Boodle*, The Clean moved to Christchurch/Ōtautahi. They briefly returned to Grey Lynn in Auckland and the Scout Hall to record with Knox and Hood their next EP for Flying Nun, *Great Sounds Great, Good Sounds Good, So So Sounds So-So, Bad Sounds Bad, Rotten Sounds Rotten!* and three more songs for a future single. Flying Nun put out *Great Sounds Great* in May and peaked at Number 4 in the charts, topping *Boodle* (though its tenure was a more modest nine weeks). Not long after its release, The Clean disbanded, citing exhaustion. Touring incessantly across Aotearoa over the previous eighteen months had taken some of the joy out of playing, and it risked becoming rote. Hamish said at the time, 'it just seemed right for a change … and we felt a little weighed down by the idea of The Clean'.[20]

However, the band had not entirely called it quits. In August, they reformed in Christchurch to open for The Fall at the start of the latter's first New Zealand tour, a notorious gig that was part of a more notorious tour.[21] Fall singer Mark E. Smith said of The Clean's performance that night: 'They got a very hard time – all these thugs in the front row started throwing bottles 'n' that, and they just walked off… They should've really got into it, probably would've been better'.[22] Their final single, 'Getting Older,' dropped in October, the title of which and the catalogue number, LAST 1, summed things up. They properly closed this chapter with a farewell gig in Ōtautahi in November with The Stones. Chris Knox later said of The Clean's import and split, they were 'the first completely original New Zealand band to get any success and it killed them. Which is pretty normal'.[23]

Big soft punch

On the heels of the success of *Boodle*, Flying Nun started to make its mark. Sales of *Boodle* went beyond everyone's expectations, providing a decent financial cushion to subsidize subsequent releases. Roger, on the advice of The Clean, assembled four up-and-coming Dunedin acts: The Stones, The Chills, Sneaky Feelings and The Verlaines. The bands, who shared a rehearsal space at the Regent Theatre in Dunedin, travelled to Christchurch to record with Knox and Hood on the TEAC, who had set up in various friends' flats. This was to serve as a label/city sampler of sorts for Dunedin. The EP format, alongside the 7-inch single, was Roger's preference as they could be recorded, pressed and released quickly (neither are the most economical formats). The collection has no official title. It simply went by the band names *The Chills, The Stones,*

The Verlaines and *Sneaky Feelings*, a four-sided, double 12-inch EP with each side dedicated to one of the bands (where the bands also contributed their artwork). As a city sampler, it's an aural snapshot of Dunedin's music scene, committing to vinyl four outfits that would be seen as the successors to The Enemy and The Clean. Though the bands are very different in sound, the EP shortly became iconic, nicknamed not long after its release as the smaller mouthful, *The Dunedin Double.* This concision also lends greater canonical weight to the supposed 'Sound' coming out of the city.[24]

With nearly twenty releases in 1982 alone, Flying Nun was prolific while still abiding by its DIY credo. An in-house graphic designer was initially considered but quickly dispensed with, and bands were given a more significant say over the art and design for their releases, much like The Clean on *Boodle.* Musicians and their friends often promoted releases and gigs, from creating and pasting up concert posters to getting records in the shops and on student radio. The liner notes for the 1985 label compilation *Tuatara*, written by Roy Colbert, recall that the records in those days were 'transported from one town to the next in a band's rattling Bedford, carried processionally through city streets by a series of untrained hands to be deposited on records shop counters with apologies for losing the invoice'.[25] (Later, the distribution would become more organized and centralized in Christchurch, with Hamish in charge.) This informal approach carried over into artists' relationships with the label, which didn't hinge on any legally binding obligation. At the time, no contracts were signed; everything was done verbally, and financing for recording varied from artist to artist. Bands could come and go as they pleased, though, in the early days, most stayed. It was *ad hoc* and fit for creative purpose, stressing the personal over the professional, an artist-centred, (mainly) artist-run approach that had built into its core an appealing sense of distance from the mainstream industry. It ran as a loose cooperative, valuing art over commerce. Here was a mode of musical production where artists didn't see themselves as alienated from their labour; on the contrary, it was very much a hands-on (sometimes an all-hands-on) process of music-making, from recording to packaging to promoting, fostering an intimate autonomy in a collective endeavour that reinforced a like-mindedness among a faction of creatively inclined people. Robert sums up how that period felt and what made it valuable to those involved, as well as what it made possible:

> We showed it could be done on the bands' terms, and Flying Nun were releasing stuff as fast as their money would allow. The bands did a lot of the work themselves, organizing the tours and promotion. Flying Nun pretty much released most stuff that the bands recorded, i.e., I don't think they turned much down, even though some of the recordings were cheap and basic, but of course this was part of the charm, it was all about the songs and approach. There was a lot of collaboration and cross pollination between the bands, people being in more than one band, sharing gear etc.[26]

The Clean left an indispensable legacy and gave Flying Nun the push it needed to carry on. While the label's flagship band had dissolved, it and the South Island sounds it aimed to represent sallied forth, encouraged by what The Clean had done. How this would manifest, the size and scope of what was to become of the band, the label and the provincial city of Dunedin and its music scene as a cultural phenomenon would go well beyond what anyone could have imagined.

4   Great sounds great

The Dunedin Sound is the sound of honesty. — **MARTIN PHILLIPPS (THE CHILLS)**[1]

The 'Dunedin Sound'. That *sound*, soon to be *the* sound. A shorthand, as inclusive as it is exclusive in summing up a musical moment that put an unassuming South Island city (and later Aotearoa) on the map. To some ears, it's a real sound, a readily identifiable set of sonic signifiers based on a style of play. This new musical vernacular mixed jangle and drone (and the occasional off-key vocals), the shared musical influences and the 'lo-fi' timbre of the recordings. To others, it's a mode of production raised to a way of life, an ethos, informal and low-key, where artists have greater control over their music-making, infusing it with authenticity and 'honesty', as Martin Phillipps suggests. The 'Sound' also alluded to a social form: a South Island scene where artists worked together in a cultural space they made their own, a regionally dispersed community bound together through their love of music and their mutual disdain for mainstream music industries and institutions (and sometimes Auckland and Australia). It also found its visual, sonic and discursive shape through media like newspapers, zines, radio and television. And this web of mediations, for many of those who were implicated in it, willingly or not, led to the myth's fabulation, taken up by some as an epithet directed at those who use it as a catchall and who fail to see the diversity of musicians, sounds and cities that this 'Sound' includes and excludes. The multifarious elements that gave it its peculiar shape are very much what Georgina Born refers to as a musical assemblage, a 'particular combination of mediations (sonic, discursive, visual, artefactual, technological, social, temporal) characteristic of a certain musical culture and historical period'.[2] This hangs together in a manner that gives it a kind of cultural purchase and lingering significance of the very sort the 'Dunedin Sound' acquired.

Tell me why

The provenance of the term 'Dunedin Sound' is not entirely clear. Roger Shepherd once claimed it, but it shows up early in print through a band interview around the time of the release of *Boodle* with Wellington scribe Dave Maclennan in the music mag *In Touch*. Asked if 'there is such a thing as a distinctive New Zealand sound?' David replies, 'No, but I think there's a Dunedin sound'.[3] It's an imprecise reference as it's unclear what that sound *is*, but it is *something*. Not long after that, there is a shift in articles from the singular 'a' to a definitive 'the' in the media. An example becomes the exemplar, hardening into a general descriptor henceforth, a point of inflexion on its way to becoming myth in Barthes's sense. It was contentious almost at once as many artists, critics and others noted, then and since, in trying to qualify or puncture the myth, some of the bands lumped in with the 'Dunedin Sound' were not, in fact, from Dunedin. And Flying Nun, the label supposedly filling its roster with bands that shared in the sound, was founded and based in Christchurch (later Auckland, but never Dunedin). These details seemed to matter little. It stuck.

Musically, the sound was (and is) often referred to as the play of strum and drone music, a mix of melody and white noise. Graeme Downes of The Verlaines, who settled into an academic career as a music lecturer some years later, sees value in making a musicological claim for specific sonic qualities. For him, some bands at the time 'projected a similar sound: trebly highly reverberant guitars, and partial barre chords with jangling or droning open strings', a sound evident across *Boodle*. Downes suggests that there were 'shared compositional strategies relating to form … a tendency to use irregular phrase structures, polymodality and a tendency towards purely musical discourse'.[4] With a knowing wink and a nod, this was parodied by the band Crystal Zoom, who released a single, 'Dunedin Sound on 45' (Flying Nun, 1985), in the medley style of Stars on 45, featuring David Kilgour and Martin Phillipps, quoting themselves and their musical peers, including The Verlaines.[5]

Others tie the 'Dunedin Sound' to a mode of production, the cheap and cheerful thriftiness of those early four-track recording sessions, conveying a live-ness unadulterated by post-production meddling.[6] John Dix, in his history of rock'n'roll in New Zealand, *Stranded in Paradise*, sums this up succinctly as the 'philosophy that the Flying Nun-Knox-Hood school introduced' in that 'young bands should avoid technological overkill; the argument being that up-market recordings can't capture an inexperienced band's sound as it really is. The message is, let the recorded sound develop as the band matures. The Flying Nun catalogue is filled with classic examples'.[7] In Dix's reading, echoed by others, those first recordings are chronicles, brimming with a riveting immediacy that sets up an unadulterated through line between purity of intent and musical execution. The recording should not be embossed with overdubs; otherwise, it risks dimming the sonic verité borne of a (mostly) live performance in the studio. This led people to refer to Flying Nun's 'lo-fi' sound on those early recordings, a timbral quality that became another hallmark of the myth.

Unsurprisingly, many of those involved in the scene, including musicians who supposedly fell under the umbrella term the 'Dunedin Sound', have opinions on it (most are critical, though some are ambivalent). Considering that moniker at the time, George Kay (writing for *Rip It Up*) suggests that 'sentimentality for garage/primitive sound coupled with journalistic laziness have been responsible for coining and creating the "Dunedin Sound" myth'.[8] David weighed in more recently, seeing it as nothing but a handy media term that fails to note the differences between the bands. 'It's a media thing, they like to name things', he says:

> All the original bands, Clean, Verlaines, Sneakys, Chills, Stones
> were all quite different really, though I guess the Stones were
> the most Clean like. It was a very exciting and vibrant scene
> by say 1982, the build-up which seemed to be happening
> since The Enemy performed in '77 was the most interesting
> period. You can trace the Dunedin scene to about ten people,
> all friends, all music freaks, hanging together in the mid 70s.[9]

Robert also saw it as the media trying to package up something neatly, suggesting 'reviewers and journalists loved having a label to put on things whether using it in a positive or negative way, for better or worse', agnostically noting 'it was a very well used term and gave the general public a reference point'. Reflecting on this in greater detail, he adds it did get muddled at times and didn't always ring true for the few it presumed to represent:

> The sound of the bands was quite broad really, so the label
> didn't really cover everyone. A few of the things the bands had

in common were singer songwriters leading the band, a lot more guitars than keyboards, no drum solos (haha), a certain lack of stage delivery of presence, i.e. maybe introduce the song '..here is a new one..' get it going then somehow end the song, oh and of course jangly guitars. This was in the live situation, on record it was a little more worked out in terms of endings and starts. With the recordings the bands would often produce themselves and usually oversee the mixing, there were just enough engineers to go round, not many studios so sometimes the bands would set up in any space and bring some gear in to make the recording happen, of course this changed over time as more studios came into being. Some people resented being lumped together under 'the Dunedin Sound' but at the time it didn't seem like a huge deal. I feel it was more after the 90s that artists mentioned not being happy with the term.[10]

Robert and David see how the myth emerges through a scene of like-minded individuals working in collective purpose, singling out how the media latches on to something that serves a story, as Scott suggests (the lazy journos Kay also refers to). Artists were sharing rehearsal, performance and recording spaces, as Robert reminds us, so there is a social fact that shapes the ecosystem of the scene, but it still doesn't do justice to what was happening at the time.

Shayne Carter (Bored Games/The Double Happys/ Straitjacket Fits/Dimmer) resents being 'lumped into' that Sound. He offers a pointed take in his memoir, *Dead People I Have Known* (2019). He's wearied of telling the Flying Nun story. 'It's like copying someone else's card', he says, '(t)he facts are all there on Wikipedia, and it's a tale that's been told a million times, always bent around the phrase "Dunedin Sound", which is a term of convenience that some journalist once used and all the others copied'. For Carter (echoing David here), the myth diminishes the diversity of people and sounds it's meant to refer to, as the bands 'resented being lumped together, because it never acknowledged the disparate characters we were, each with our own pig-headed vision of what rock'n'roll should be'.[11]

Engineer/producer/artist Stephen Kilroy shares a similar view. He set up Fish Street Studios in Dunedin in the early 1990s, overseeing the recording of some of the later Clean records, members' solo albums and later waves of Flying Nun bands (such as The 3Ds). Kilroy echoes Carter's reading, suggesting that the 'Dunedin Sound' was problematic for several reasons:

> There were several things in the myth about how it came about … For a great musical culture to exist, you need good practice spaces, cheap rents, good record shops and a good music shop and that creates the community. So the 'Dunedin Sound' become a thing that people could put in a record bin and it became a moniker. It was journalistic laziness as well, because you compare Sneaky Feelings to Snapper both beside each other in the record bin, but they're a million miles away from each other in terms of their sound. So, it was a convenient moniker, but then again, with the Liverpool sound they probably went through the same thing. Gerry and the Pacemakers were not all that different from The Beatles, but there were certainly other things happening there that were different.[12]

Those who were part of the scene at the time carved out a cultural space that fostered a diversity of sounds and practices, proactively creating social and cultural conditions that allowed them to flourish. As Kilroy suggests, the media, from local newspapers to music mags to national weeklies, framed the myth in ways that winnowed that diverse cohort of bands and their respective sounds into a narrower box (or record bin in this case). For him, it's hard to reconcile how Sneaky Feelings, who were avowedly pop-oriented and often saw themselves as excluded from the 'Sound' and the scene, can be so cavalierly catalogued in record shops alongside Snapper, whose songs were built around Peter Gutteridge's distortion-driven guitar squeals and acerbic Suicide-like keyboard pulses.[13]

How the 'Dunedin Sound' is discursively produced suggests something more at work, beyond the barre chords, well-appointed 1960s and 1970s musical references and a preference for lo-fi timbres, something beyond the jangle and drone. As Oli Wilson (currently a member of The Chills) and Mike Holland note, 'the significance of this "sound" is more related to Dunedin artists' subversion of dominant commercial music industry and recording practices – grounded in a specific time and ideological space – than its musicological or sonic uniqueness'.[14] Graeme Downes put his ethnomusicology hat on and offered a subtler read of the significance of the 'Sound', which also points to the predominantly Pākehā, white male-dominated music culture it valorized. '(T)he Dunedin sound represents a cultural nationalism of a sort. The bands tended to eschew cultural influences to which – as pakeha [sic] New Zealanders generally and Dunedinites specifically – they felt no cultural ownership'. He notes that 'Afro-American influences, such as blues, soul or funk, for example, were largely avoided'. 'The remaining, greatly diminished, stylistic pool' he suggests, 'arguably contains folk music, urban white rock (anything from the Beatles to the Velvet Underground) and classical music (both of the Western variety and, possibly, via the orientalism of the Beatles and the Velvets, Indian)'.[15]

Downes's reference to cultural nationalism is another dimension of the myth that accrued to it over time. In its earliest days, the common bond was more a subcultural alterity, founded on a mutual love of bands that formed around those shared musical references. Added to this was a collective disdain for what was happening elsewhere (particularly Auckland but also Australia). Some years later, though, it gets touted as *the* sound of New Zealand, evincing a *New Zealand-ness* that came to be valorized nationally and internationally. Matthew Bannister (of Sneaky Feelings, also now an academic) echoes Downes's reading, though he's more pointed in describing its organizing logic. He similarly locates the 'Sound' in something sociologically significant, taking the form of banal cultural nationalism.[16] It's centred around a particular ethnos and ethos that settler cultures in Aotearoa are wont to embrace as an identity marker:

> Punk/indie discourse in Aotearoa/New Zealand and the establishment of the Dunedin Sound was ultimately more about local 'settler society'-inflected DIY creativity and aesthetics than direct transplantation of UK class-based punk ethos in the construction of a localised definition of national identity through music. In NZ, discourses of punk/indie autonomy 'worked' partly because they fed into and assuaged local settler discourses of identity, which were historically identified with white masculinity. The identification of indie music with local scenes was then reproduced at a national and international level – the Dunedin Sound became the New Zealand sound, supporting a construction of local music as mainly by white, male South Islanders.[17]

What happened in Dunedin at the time was a product of historical and geographical circumstances, combined with techniques and technologies, discourses and practices, all arrayed in a captivating assemblage, as Russell or Born might have it. Taken together, and in the case of what happened in and around Dunedin, this clustering articulates a myth New Zealand often tells itself about autonomy and independence. These are constantly referred to in relation to the city's supposed isolation from the rest of the country and, more so, the world. In this telling of the tale, ex-centricity leads to eccentricity, a handicap that becomes a mark of distinction, framed in familiar terms that could be scaled up so it could be the nation's sound.[18]

Regardless of its rightness or wrongness, the 'Dunedin Sound' was loosed upon Aotearoa and soon the world. Many bands and artists it apparently spoke of and for, whether they wanted it to or not, were slowly separated from shaping it, whatever 'it' was. The narrative was no longer theirs to control. Uprooted from the material and sociomusical practices it purports to represent, the 'Sound' circulates through the mediascape as synecdoche, a vague part standing in for a fuzzy whole. At an earlier phase of its life, its subcultural power rested on how it expressed its distance from the mainstream recording industry, a counterhegemonic mode of making music that sketched out a different moral universe and evoked a distinctive structure of feeling. It retains those elements as potent signifiers, to varying degrees, but is now distanced from its point of origin in a real time and a real place, reassembled into a differently charged set of temporal and spatial relationships and associations. As Bannister notes, the 'Dunedin Sound' took discursive shape more problematically as *the* New Zealand sound, first regionally and then globally.

Modern rock

> When anyone writes about New Zealand music, they mean
> Flying Nun records … In its prime, Flying Nun's embrace
> of all post-punk's manifestations – exquisite psych-pop,
> cantankerous quasi-goth, warped folk, experimental synth
> warfare – meant it was New Zealand's Rough Trade, Factory,
> Postcard and Mute rolled into one … What came to be
> known as the Dunedin Sound was an amalgam of jangly
> garage-pop invested with a spooky, otherworldly touch – as
> if being on the other side of the world meant the music was
> played upside down.
>
> – Martin Aston[19]

Aston, a Brit who in the 1980s once served as The Chills UK
publicist, writing in *The Guardian* in 2009, offers a salient take
on the 'Dunedin Sound' a quarter of a century later and a world
away. Some of his genre tags might be hard to parse, but name-
checking the kindred-spirit labels helps. All from the UK, it's a
litany that solicits an agreeable nod of acknowledgement from
the in-the-know reader as to the type of aesthetic and mode
of DIY production that drove Flying Nun. While written with
apparent fondness, the offhanded opening line exemplifies
the mystifying way the country and label are conflated
around a particular mythical moment. In 2009, would it be
disingenuous to ask why Fat Freddy's Drop, purveyors of the
'Wellington Sound', or OMC are not seen as ambassadors for
New Zealand music?[20] Both had international profiles, and
OMC had a global chart hit with 'How Bizarre' (Huh Records,
1996). More to the point, in 2009, Flying Nun was still releasing
music from New Zealand and overseas artists. The allusion to a

label 'in its prime' imagines a prelapsarian moment when Flying Nun and its music were perceived as genuinely authentic and not mired in the dramas of global media conglomerate mergers and acquisitions. That the music sounded like it was 'played upside down', even if a clichéd antipodal reference (see *The Simpsons* in Australia for similar jibes), only added to the tenacious appeal of its lo-fi uncanniness.

A year later, Christchurch's *The Press* summed up the overseas impact of Flying Nun and the Dunedin Sound by calling on Jonathon Poneman, co-founder of Sub-Pop Records (also cited in *The Guardian* piece). Sub-Pop, saddled with its own 'sound' in the form of grunge, sometimes called the 'Seattle Sound', helped launch the careers of Nirvana, Mudhoney and L7, among others. Closer to the present, the label has represented New Zealand bands such as Auckland's The Beths, Christchurch's Pickle Darling and Wellington comedy duo Flight of the Conchords, among others. Poneman's thoughts are telling:

> The early Flying Nun bands [Poneman] explains, were making their own version of the 'pop-informed indie rock' that American college radio wanted to hear. It caught on. Dunedin became a 'regional scene', on a par with places like Athens, Georgia, which spawned REM, and the Pacific Northwest, birthplace of the Seattle sound … Records were intercontinental semaphores, a way of conjuring up a place or a region. I had a conception of what Dunedin must be like – beautiful, remote and crawling with great bands.[21]

Flying Nun and Dunedin, musical practice and the place are all conflated here. The fact that the label and several bands were based in Christchurch is again overlooked. In Poneman's take, the label and the city's scene produced a DIY toolkit. The bands are ambassadors for an imagined fantasyland of independent music-making 'crawling with bands' that aligned easily with better-known quantities such as Athens or Seattle, scenes that also sat on the margins of the typical musical centres and did their own thing (until they, too, succumbed to the tractor-beam pull of the majors).

For Aston, Poneman and many others outside the country, the 'Dunedin Sound' is a handy, albeit attenuated, abbreviation for independent music coming from Aotearoa. The circulation of the myth beyond New Zealand's borders reconstitutes and reaffirms any number of interrelated practices that members of other indie scenes around the world can see themselves reflected in, from a mode of production, the spirit of voluntarism, the image of a place that is geographically and musically isolated, an upstart scene and stalwart label that supports them, to a supposed signature sound. Colin McLeay suggests that these are ancillary to what is going on concerning how the 'Dunedin Sound' functions. Unmoored from its sociospatial context, now a floating signifier, it's valued as a set of connotations and associations oriented to another time and place, a frame of reference/reverence Aston and Poneman share. Dunedin is conjured up as 'a place where everything is "real" and the music is not tainted by the falsity of technology and commercial pressure.'[22] 'What is crucial is that Dunedin, and the Dunedin sound', McLeay suggests, 'are considered to represent the core value of community in music production. The construction of a cultural history of Dunedin music by musicians, fans and critics has been dominated by a desire for a sense of nostalgia and community.'[23] He points out that the weight placed on what was happening in the late 1970s and early 1980s in a provincial city at the bottom of a country at the bottom of the world as a cultural space may be 'more significant as a myth than a "reality"'. However, 'there is little doubt that the Dunedin sound continues as a coverall to describe the local popular music of Dunedin'.[24] That assessment, written some thirty years ago, resonates in myriad ways even today.

For those implicated in it, the 'Dunedin Sound' inserted them into a discursive envelope containing many different and contested dimensions. Several artists initially associated with it disown it as a media contrivance, as a rhetorical sleight-of-hand that elides the many differences between bands, their sounds and the places they came from. Over time, it has matured into a polyvalent myth that still holds sway. No other New Zealand scene, musical or otherwise, continues to be as celebrated, criticized, anthologized, archived, reissued, reassessed, lionized, eulogized, scrutinized and, of course, mythologized. This persistence continues to play out in contemporary Dunedin and Aotearoa in intriguing and often confounding ways.

5 Trapped in amber

The term 'Dunedin Sound' still had cultural capital … People are still interested in what is coming out of this town based on the reputation of what happened 30 years ago. **– RICHARD LEY-HAMILTON (SINGER FROM DUNEDIN BAND MALES)**[1]

And finally, a quick word to those thinking of including the words 'Flying Nun' in their reviews. Please mail your review to the burning core of the sun and then set yourself on fire and die. Thanks, and enjoy the album. **– CENTRE NEGATIVE, EXCERPT FROM 'IN'**[2]

In 2018, to commemorate Ed Sheeran's three-concert stint over Easter Weekend in the city, Dunedin Enterprise, a division of the City Council tasked with implementing economic development strategies and 'destination marketing', sponsored the painting of a mural of the singer in the city's central entertainment hub, The Octagon. Not surprisingly, this was met with a lot of teeth-gnashing, letters-to-the-editor cries of taxpayer-funded wastage and claims it insulted the city's rich musical culture and heritage. The media weighed in, and pundits and locals alike took umbrage, horrified at what most took to be a tone-deaf gaffe and an ignorant diss of local music history. Dunedin musical elder statesmen were approached to opine. Martin Phillipps of The Chills demurely stated, 'I've got nothing really against Ed', noting he 'would go to Sheeran's concert if there was a free ticket available'. However, he continues, 'the mural made Dunedin look like a small-town lacking culture'. Graeme Downes posited that in 'a decade's time people will ask "who's that?" I suppose'. And Roger Shepherd cheekily suggested, '(Sheeran) is a well-known Wellington lover. I guess that Dunedin show generated the impetus to paint him on a wall. I'm pretty sure bands like The Enemy, The Clean, Verlaines, and The Chills also played Dunedin shows … so I'm looking forward to seeing them up on the wall'.[3]

Of what relevance is Sheeran to Dunedin? Wasn't there a more deserving local artist (or band) to showcase? The Council suggested the mural 'would further reinforce Dunedin's reputation as a creative and innovative city, when it comes to major events'.[4] 'Our intention is to leverage this work as a key part of our Dunedin brand activity in the lead-up and during the Ed Sheeran concerts', a Council official stated.[5] The furore continued for a few days and then faded from view, but the mural remains. Surprisingly, or perhaps not, it has only suffered minor defilement. This may be because the piece is hardly public facing; you need to seek it out, given its placement above an entranceway to a car park in front of a now-defunct night club on a side street in the Octagon that acts as more of a delivery lane than a widely trafficked thoroughfare. With some irony, however, for a few years it was just metres away from one of the city's hip bakery cafés, Side On (which closed in late 2023), named after The Clean track from their follow-up EP to *Boodle*, *Great Sounds Great*.

This vignette could well be a contemporary urban allegory. It's instructive on several issues the city faces as the Council and Dunedin Enterprise are busy entrepreneurializing its cultural life, harnessing it for economic growth (and, for some, seemingly oblivious to the musical legacy on their doorstep). At the same time, it affords some closure by way of a reflection on the legacy of the *Boodle* EP, The Clean, Flying Nun and the myth of the 'Dunedin Sound'. There is a curious spectre we're left with when thinking through how this convergence of band, place, sound and label do (and don't) underpin Dunedin's cultural identity and independent music-making in Aotearoa and how those legacies are understood and valued, by whom, in what contexts and to what purpose. The myth has spun out in multiple directions, taken on manifold forms and put to very different ends. In one incarnation, it invokes reckons, reminisces and wishes that it would go away. In another, the 'Dunedin Sound' has morphed into an urban amenity, a cultural residue sopped up into a handy reference pool used to bolster civic pride or mobilized as a branding tool in appeals to discerning tourists and investors. In this, it has become a shared semiotic resource that can be drawn from to tend to the city's musical history and cultural heritage, which includes fighting for the cultural value of landmark venues threatened with closure to the preservation of the material culture that threatens to decay or disappear. The myth may have been abused, but it still has its uses.

Hold on to the rail

Best to rewind here to provide some broader historical context for the current situation and offer some thoughts on how and why the myth of the 'Dunedin Sound' fails to fade. Not long after its auspicious start, Flying Nun's clutch of fiercely independent bands expanded rapidly. At its core was its DIY ethos, of the sort Bruce Russell refers to as crucial to music-making in Aotearoa. That central disposition was also shared by New Zealanders at large, referred to colloquially as 'Kiwi ingenuity' or the 'number 8-wire attitude'. The latter alludes to a gauge of fencing wire that became ubiquitous among early farmers in Aotearoa due to its cheapness and flexibility. Its adaptability allowed it to go beyond its use as fencing and put it to a range of other practical uses around the farm. As practice and attitude, it's tied to the colonial settlers making the most of what they had in front of them. It has long shaped (and continues to shape) discourses around innovation and creativity in New Zealand. In this crucial respect, DIY is not the preserve of Flying Nun or the bands on its roster; instead, it's shared by many in Aotearoa, particularly Pakehā, as a pragmatic way of dealing with the circumstances of geography, getting by with what's at hand and making the most of life under the tyranny of distance. However, the rise of independent, do-it-yourself music shadows an ominous development in Aotearoa, where that DIY sensibility and the cleverness at its core is tried and tested throughout the 1980s (and afterwards).

Complications

In 1985, not long after Flying Nun was up and running, the new Labour government under David Lange and the then Minister of Finance, Roger Douglas, in line with many governments across the world, began to implement neoliberal policies that fundamentally altered the social, cultural and economic structures of Aotearoa. As the protectionist approach of earlier governments and crucial support mechanisms of the social welfare state were swept away in favour of the market-led reforms, New Zealand, from this point forward, became a grand social experiment for neoliberalism in all its guises, from Thatcherite to Blairite and beyond.[6] In a deregulated, free market context where entrepreneurialism wasn't only a goal but a survival strategy, as a trope fundamental to the discourses shaping national, specifically settler colonial, identity, 'Kiwi ingenuity' acquired a different meaning. A pioneering DIY myth that underwrote many of the stories this settler nation told itself for so long (not unproblematically) was now being yoked to a different set of problematic imperatives. In an increasingly competitive context organized around the logic of the free market, notions like DIY and 'Kiwi ingenuity' were reimagined, serving as alibis for and accomplices to neoliberalism. As S. H. Franklin has argued, there is historical precedence that enabled neoliberalism to colonize the national imaginary in this way, owing to the peculiarities of the New Zealand welfare state itself:

> (T)he risk taking, independent small businessman has remained a powerful image in the welfare state … an image reinforced by the economic reality that much of our export trade is based on owner-operated farms and a psychological reality – the desire and ambition of many New Zealanders to be their own boss … an ambition which the policies of the welfare state have enabled many to fulfil.[7]

Throughout the 1980s and well into the following decades, that powerful myth of New Zealand's inventive colonial settler, sometimes referred to also as 'the Kiwi battler', morphed into the incentivized entrepreneur, recalibrating that 'psychological reality' so that ambition and aspiration could be translated into cultural scripts and metrics that individuals were encouraged to follow and, better yet, measure themselves and others by. 'Creativity' and 'innovation' were latched onto as buzzwords, embraced as a worthy national lexicon, expressing a sensibility that set New Zealand and New Zealanders apart in the global marketplace. They form the mantra of what some refer to as the nation's 'innovation ecosystem'.[8] While that term might have some mystifyingly organic connotations, the free market remains the pervasive metaphor, and market-led reforms were an essential driver of this ascendent myth, one with profound material, social and cultural consequences.

Neoliberalism also reshaped urban imaginaries throughout Aotearoa. As central government resourcing shrank, city councils had to find innovative ways to secure their economic futures. Seeking creative solutions meant they regarded urban culture as a potential resource. Like many other urban centres worldwide, New Zealand's cities had to entrepreneurialize to find that 'point of distinction' in a global market made reliant on the symbolic and cultural capital associated with urban attractors like the 'experience economy', a 'socioeconomic system where aesthetic experiences, rather than goods or services, form the basis for generating value', implemented in such a way as to make their cities 'eventful'.[9] Cultural consumption was a growth area. In these cities, words like 'creative' and 'innovative' become part of the vocabulary employed by branding teams, an idiom critical to a promotional arsenal and entrenched in urban development strategies and cultural policies. The aim is to draw in well-heeled tourists and investors, local and international. This led to the rise of arts festivals and other cultural events, whereby a city's cultural capital could be transformed into economic capital. Cities had to learn how to better manage and market their cultural resources in the form of cultural commodities.[10]

Orvar Löfgren asks what the consequences are for cities that embrace this approach: 'What happens when a cultural heritage becomes a brand, when a city is turned into an event, a commodity into an experience, a way of life into a style … or everyday life into design?'[11] In Aotearoa, with an economy heavily reliant on tourist dollars, the neoliberalization of cities manifests with countless festivals and events organized around cultural consumption, from food to film to literature to arts and music. In this context, having a music scene or band of renown has a degree of utility, the kind of cultural amenity with marketing and monetizing potential. This could involve mobilizing a city's musical histories regarding notable artists or scenes and packaging them into consumable cultural assets through events or experiences.

Dunedin's long-term spatial plan makes clear there's a place in policy and in the future for the city's musical history, with the myth recast again, now anointed as its own *genre*: 'Cultural icons, such as the "Dunedin Sound" music genre, remain in the nation's psyche while new work is made by the eclectic and diverse range of artists who live here'.[12] An early example of tapping into the psyche, selling the city and packaging up the 'Sound' came through the Otago Arts Festival. In 2001, the organizers had packaged the Dunedin Sound in its festival line-up (which included a concert by The Clean). The programmers noted that for 'rock aficionados of all ages … the Dunedin sound is a cult market with an international following. It's music which has put Dunedin on the map since the 1980s'.[13] Classifying the sound as a 'cult market' suggests it has matured into its mythical status with the right kind of connoisseurist appeal, evolved into a signifier of urban cool such that it appeals to the desired and discerning taste cultures an arts festival imagines as its core demographic.

The Dunedin Sound continues to circulate with a promiscuity that speaks to its versatility and pliability. The city's previous role in the region's extractive industry, mining, has been transformed in a thoroughly contemporary, postmodern revamp, with the material replaced by the symbolic as a resource primed for excavation. In this capacity, the 'Sound' persists as a still-useful repository, its depths plumbed by diverse interests, from musicians to archivists to city councillors to urban brand management teams. In its most banal form, it's been turned into a City Council-sponsored Spotify playlist on The DunedinNZ Spotify channel, which 'aims to evoke nostalgia and stimulate curiosity about the city', playing fast and loose with periodization, however, 'by compiling playlists of the "Dunedin Sound" from the past and present', with the music to 'be played across council venues and events … on outdoor stages or as on-hold music'.[14] Beyond hold music and its curious stimulations, Flying Nun and the 'Sound' have also inspired specific beers, a more obvious fit between the country's fertile DIY craft beer scene and the kindred indie spirit of the scene. In 2011, on the occasion of Flying Nun's thirtieth anniversary, Dunedin-based brewery Emerson's Beers introduced a line dedicated to the bands on the label, which included The Verlaines (Bird Dog Pale), a tribute to the Chills (Rolling Moon), and The Clean, with Tally Ho!.[15] Closer to the present, the Dunedin Sound has been the impetus for an upgraded high-spec mixing console at Otago University's music programme (where Graeme Downes was once based). Stephen Stedman, the studio manager, refers to Toy Love, The Chills, The Verlaines and others as part of the rationale for the upgrade: 'The explosion of music in Dunedin was a contributing factor to us having a contemporary music program at Otago, which led to us having this studio, because we needed somewhere to run that program'.[16]

Back in the day

A recent minor publishing boom has shifted the myth into different registers, sometimes contemplative, reflective and occasionally revisionist. There are memoirs from some critical figures, such as Roger Shepherd's *In Love with These Times* and Shayne Carter's *Dead People I Have Known*, which add their own nuances and stances regarding the myth. These sit alongside Ian Chapman's photo-essay book *The Dunedin Sound: Some Disenchanted Evening* (2016), Matt Goody's *Needles and Plastic: Flying Nun Records, 1981–1988* (2022) and Richard Langston's *Pull Down the Shades: Garage Fanzine 1984–86* (2023). Like Shepherd and Carter, this trifecta of publications goes some way to addressing the myth differently, adding all-important minutiae to the musical world that existed in Aotearoa at the time.

Chapman's book is a visual record of the bands associated with the 'Dunedin Sound' as he frames it. This is an idiosyncratic take that stretches the rubric to include those that might be understood as 'canonical' but also to artists that played on the experimental, free-form, noisy side of the street, such as Plagal Grind and The Dead C.[17] The focus is also only on Dunedin-based bands. *Needles and Plastic* followed a few years later, mining similar territory with an organizing logic built not around the city or the 'Sound' but only Flying Nun releases. A meticulous account of all the singles released during the years the label was based in the South Island (the cut-off being the label's move to Auckland at the end of the 1980s), Goody offers up a sumptuous detailed encyclopaedic tome, weaving together many stories, filled with vital trivia on the making-of for the classic Flying Nun releases, including *Boodle*. Given its label wide scope, he also gives equal weight to other singles and bands that otherwise have not been considered 'canonical', a reminder of Flying Nun's more catholic inclinations. Like Chapman, the book draws heavily on the visual culture that is a distinctive part of the label, with hundreds of personal photos, gig posters, album art and other ephemera included. *Pull Down the Shades*, Langston's book, is a compilation of the six-issue run of *Garage* zine between 1984 and 1986, of which he was the founder and a central scribe. The issues sit alongside commentary from those actively making music at the time. While not shy about playing favourites – The Clean and its members are well-represented – like Goody's book, Langston's collection illustrates how diverse and energetic the music and scenes in Aotearoa were at the time. All are substantive and invaluable documents in their own way. These (re)collections provide a vitally important public service in assembling material that might otherwise be lost to time, with most of it coming from their collections or from the artists and participants active then. A powerful sense of connection, intimacy and personality is displayed here. They also draw from a period of musical history once again memorialized and anthologized, albeit in reiterations appended with crucial details and gradations that the ensuing decades smoothed out or erased, but at no less risk of reconstituting the myth by pulling the focus back again to a well-worn musical time and place.

Timepiece

The institutionalization of the Dunedin Sound shares in the spirit of preservation of these anthologies. However, a concerted effort exists to maintain that heritage according to a different set of imperatives. In some cases, this is about bringing history into view in service to public edification. An early example was staged at the Toitū Otago Settlers Museum in 2012. At the time, Martin Phillipps said, 'It's great that they are treating it as history now – what we all did'.[18] The show included David Kilgour's famed Ibanez guitar, an amp from Robert, and a TEAC four-track of the type Chris Knox and Doug Hood used to record The Clean and other Flying Nun bands.

Further education and edification can be found in the musical event *Tally Ho!*, where the city's Southern Sinfonia Orchestra performed symphonic renditions of some of those early Dunedin sounds (which included contributions from musicians Martin Phillipps and David Kilgour). Organized with The Verlaines's Graeme Downes, Roy Colbert saw these events (three in total) as a way to showcase what he thought was an oversight. 'It's my feeling they haven't really got across to the general public … It's sort of a garage music, a cult music, so I thought let's present the songs to the general public in an accessible or different way … It still hasn't reached enough people for the quality of it'.[19] Here, the institutional legitimacy associated with an orchestra in an environment that necessitated a different listening mode, the primmer bourgeois modalities required of the august symphony hall over the prosaic ambience of the pub or dive bar.

The material culture associated with the myth is preserved in places such as the Alexander Turnbull Library at the National Library in Wellington and the Hocken Collections, based at Otago University. As to the former, in 2018, Flying Nun's manager Ben Howe (whose previous label Arch Hill released music by The Clean and David Kilgour) recovered the label's master tapes. Until then, they had been untraceable. Warner Music NZ, previous owners of the catalogue, was moving house up in Auckland, and after earlier attempts to recover them turned up nothing, the tapes just appeared.[20] With the artists' permission, these were donated to the Alexander Turnbull Library. The latter was tasked with properly preserving the tapes and digitizing this material to 'ensure the long-term preservation of and access to these important recordings, allowing them to be available for remastering and reissuing, and for research purposes'.[21]

Down south, Hocken Collections, a research library, houses an archive comprising a range of ephemera associated with the Dunedin Sound, from zines to newspaper clippings, photos, live recordings (audio, visual and bootleg), cassette tapes and other materials, much of it donated by participants and fans. The purpose, says curator Amanda Mills, is 'to document the scene in-depth', and 'to contextualize the different experiences and narratives that run through the scene'.[22] In 2021, the fortieth anniversary of Flying Nun, the Hocken hosted 'Kaleidoscope World: 40 Years of Flying Nun in Dunedin', displaying a selection of their collection associated with the label and the city.[23] Like those earlier books, these institutions provide an essential service in recognizing and preserving this material, with the added benefit that they're now held as a public good.

More recently, the myth of the Dunedin Sound has stoked a curious paradox. The City Council has pointed to it as a hallmark of Ōtepoti's creative heritage, an asset they deemed attractive to tourists. It also positions the city as a vibrant cultural hub, making it increasingly attractive to real estate developers and investors who can pitch that urban buzz to discerning buyers. That same 'Sound' has simultaneously been mobilized, ironically but with utmost seriousness, as a bulwark against the consequences of the city's gentrification working in the latter constituency's interest. In 2022, consent was granted for residential housing to be built next to the Crown Hotel, host to many bands often referred to as part of the 'Dunedin

Sound'. With no requirement to properly soundproof this new build, the likelihood of complaints was thought inevitable and could have been the death knell for the legendary venue. In their fight for securing the future of the venue (and others), the advocacy group Save Dunedin Live Music (SDLM) made the case that the city had 'promoted itself for years off the back of its music scene and the Dunedin Sound' and now it's 'time for the council to put their money where their mouth is and make the necessary changes to support their local venues and artists'.[24] The SDLM campaign fed into the *Ōtepoti Live Music Action Plan*, which the City Council considered in September 2023. In their words, the aim is to build 'on the foundations of Dunedin's strong music heritage with a planned approach supporting Dunedin's music ecosystem to thrive'.[25] The Council approved the plan just a month before the closure of Dive (due to eviction), formerly the Captain Cook Tavern.

Whatever I do is right/wrong

The urban anthropologist Rolf Lindner, reflecting on the nature of myths in the city, asks, 'are mythologies in fact only really authorized through emulation, by an afterlife, just as these, in turn, lend this life substance, by entering the everyday speech, the *parole* and the habits of the inhabitants?'.[26] Myths are iterative and recursive, discursive and symbolic loops fed back into the city through those stories that it tells of itself and are told of it in books, films, music, poems, news stories, tabloids, weeklies, a polyglot of reflections, refractions and representations. These are cumulative mediations fed into the circulatory systems of cities that we might liken to folklore, but Lindner sees them instead as citylore. Citylore can act as ballast, adding gravitas to a place and contributing to its distinctive urban character. Occasionally, cities can get trapped in a myth (Lindner cites Los Angeles as an example), seduced by these cultural texts and weighed down by cumulative sedimentation. This can slow things down or ossify into a nostalgia that becomes intractable, to the detriment of those who would like to move on, to do something innovative and *out of character*.

While the City Council and any number of contemporary Dunedin bands are willing to embrace the afterlife of the myth, other artists feel unduly haunted by the 'Sound'. Those who choose to resist can resort to provocative tactics. Such is the case of the band Coyote, who in 2018 took it upon themselves to deface a telecommunications box across the street from the Captain Cook Hotel. This had been done up as a tribute to The Chills, painted by a local artist and admitted fan (the city had conscripted local artists to paint these rather mundane units into something more stylish). The duo painted their tag over The Chills' name, gleefully filming the Oedipal act and posting it on social media (the band later tagged the Ed Sheeran mural).[27] Local press was appalled. Of the ensuing media outrage, Jeremy, one half the duo, says he finds this

> obsession with the past kind of alienating … It's like, I wasn't there, I'm here now, I feel like the music we're making is better than … Well I dunno, I feel like it's really fucking good and the Dunedin sound or whatever is just all these old people obsessed with the past and it's like, yeah, cool for you guys but shut up and let us make our own contemporary scene.[28]

Another Dunedin musician, Millie Lovelock from Astro Children, speaking to the incident, echoes that sentiment:

> There was a lot of discussion like 'We wouldn't even have a music scene in Dunedin if it weren't for The Chills and how

dare these young people disrespect their elders and deface such a beautiful work of art'. So there was a division that made itself clear in the last week or so. Older people in the scene very much feel that we should all bow down to these Dunedin greats, who arguably only have one or two good songs between them, and not act out of turn.[29]

A few years later, Hannah Herchenbach considered the exclusionary power of the myth of the Dunedin Sound and Christchurch's overlooked role in servicing the scene of its South Island neighbour. Writing on the occasion of the fortieth-anniversary retrospective of Flying Nun art and design held at the Christchurch Art Gallery in 2021 (another instance of institutionalization and memorialization echoing the show hosted by the Hocken Collections), Herchenbach reminds those attending the show there's another story that's been disappeared in the myth:

> The story of the South Island rock music culture that produced Flying Nun is a spatial history of movement between towns. The flat stretch of highway that connects Christchurch and Dunedin remains unnoticed in the stories written by those on the North Island or overseas and is too obvious for those living on the South Island to point out. Yet the connection has been overlooked to the exclusion of Christchurch, and Dunedin is accepted as Flying Nun's 'spiritual home'. For some reason no one has said it yet, so I will: Dunedin acquired its rock reputation by siphoning off Christchurch's capital and claiming all the credit.[30]

This, too, is a corrective as provocation, the kind of detail that the broad strokes of the myth of the 'Dunedin Sound' often obscures. It appears to have had little effect, however. The latticework of references and texts coming from and gathering in myriad quarters – media, institutions, fans, bands, anthologies, retrospectives, archives, reissues and others, here in Aotearoa and overseas – has thickened into a dense carapace hard to pierce, making the stock-standard storyline difficult to shift. Lindner suggests that 'these cultural codings have a cumulative effect, in part the result of the process of continuous intertextual cross-reference'.[31] In the case of the Dunedin Sound, its resilience as a seemingly bottomless resource is continually replenished and revived by the numerous publications, retrospectives, gallery showings and the words and actions of interested parties (whose interests may not align), as well as by those who seek to escape it. Lindner suggests the trap can be inevitable, as 'those who want to distance themselves from what are seen as clichés involuntarily reinforce them through repetition, even if in a critical context'.[32] Those seeking to confront the myth or looking for ways out of it are dragged back into it. Gary Steel, publisher and editor of *In Touch* magazine, which gave us one of the earliest in-print instances of the 'Dunedin Sound' moniker, does just this. In a stinging review of Roger Shepherd's memoir, *In Love with These Times*, he lays out what he sees as wrong with the myth:

> (T)he idea that most of the best New Zealand music of the '80s came from Dunedin, or that Flying Nun was behind most of the best music, is a myth. For many, Flying Nun is ground zero for NZ music. But the label's prominence has sadly obscured all the great music that happened outside of its orbit, and all of the great bands that didn't quite fit its post-punk alt-rock/indie aesthetic. An aesthetic that, as viewed through the prism of that tiny Dunedin scene from which emerged bands like The Clean, The Chills and The Verlaines, requires the wearing of black jerseys and sneers at

anything commercial, or anything that doesn't jive with its sense of cool. And that idea of cool hinges on an unhealthy obsession with the Velvet Underground and Nuggets-era garage bands from the '60s. It's cheap and uncheerful and the uniform guitar jangle covers up its musical deficiencies.[33]

In castigating those who perpetuate the myth, Steel, much like Herchenbach, ends up in the paradoxical thrall of it, where even railing against it only gives it more life. As Barthes reminds us, myth is the great reanimator, as 'a language which does not want to die: it wrests from the meanings which give it its sustenance an insidious, degraded survival, it provokes in them an artificial reprieve in which it settles comfortably, it turns them into speaking corpses'.[34] This is the wily, hypnotic pull of myth. Zombie-like, myth acquires its social life and retains its cultural power parasitically by drawing in, absorbing and neutralizing criticisms, revivifying and re-centring it as the thing still being discussed. Sometimes even more so when certain parties prefer to speak ill of the undead.

6   Do your thing

Back in the day, The Clean were reviled, criticised and put down so I developed a pretty thick skin … in terms of recognition we already got it from the people that supported us. — **HAMISH KILGOUR**[1]

Having called it quits in 1982, The Clean still enjoyed an afterlife.[2] This was primarily through belated releases like the cassette compilations *Odditties* (Cleano Productions, 1983) and *Odditties 2* (Flying Nun, 1988), made up mainly of live cuts and demos, many recorded on their two-track Revox, and a live EP, *Live Dead Clean* (released in 1986, but culled from various Dunedin and Auckland gigs between 1981 and 1982). In 1987, Flying Nun launched a 'career' retrospective, *Compilation*, a sampler drawing from the band's singles and EPs, designed to capitalize on the label's widening international connections. Licensing to Normal Records, out of Germany, Au Go Go in Australia, through the label's recent UK, London-based wing, Flying Nun UK, and later the American distributor Homestead ensured *Compilation* found its way into countless independent record stores, radio stations and the collections of a global network of indie rock aficionados. This piqued interest not only in The Clean but prompted overseas fans to seek out some of the other sounds emanating from the other side of the world, giving Flying Nun, Dunedin and its 'Sound' another kind of life.

This renewed fascination was timely. To many people's surprise, The Clean reassembled in 1988 to do their first overseas gigs. Joining Robert's outfit, The Bats, in the UK for two shows, the trio dipped into the back catalogue and ran through some new songs. One of these gigs was recorded as an EP, *In-A-Live*, released through Flying Nun Europe in 1989. They went on to tour New Zealand, Australia, America and Europe and returned to the UK. They stayed on in London to record their first proper album, *Vehicle* (1990), financed by and released through Rough Trade (label head Geoff Travis caught one of their London gigs and was impressed enough to chip in with financing for the recording). Four more LPs followed, recorded at the band's own pace: *Modern Rock* (Flying Nun, 1994), *Unknown Country* (Flying Nun, 1996), *Getaway* (Merge, 2001) and what was to be their last effort, *Mr. Pop* (Arch Hill/Morr Music/Merge Records, 2009). Robert described the band as a 'part-time' affair, and David once referred to The Clean as a 'part-time hobby … sort of'.[3] Reviewing *Vehicle*, American rock critic Robert Christgau dubs them 'sporadic semi-pros … with a boyish strain about them', a sensibility that manifests on each subsequent album.[4] As part-time post-punks and South Island east-coast pop art experimentalists, these later albums still bear their signature lack of pretension, their easy way with melodic pop and rock hooks lashed together with that playfulness, humour and experimentation that has remained a constant, from 'Tally Ho!' on. Their musical references are now much harder to place, as they fossick around a sound and style audibly their own.

In the years after their last proper album, The Clean did carry on with occasional overseas and local tours. In 2014, while in Aotearoa, they were joined on stage at a few shows by founding member Peter Gutteridge, jumping in on some tunes, most notably 'Point That Thing', the very song he wrote with the Kilgours over three decades earlier. One of those performances, at Chick's Hotel in Port Chalmers on the outskirts of Dunedin, is caught on video.[5] All four of them are up on a cramped stage, Robert anchoring that iconic bassline to Hamish, hammering away at his drumkit in Mo Tucker/ motorik style and occasionally singing. David also chimes in on vocals while playing those famed barre chords to open up the song's signature chasms, filled in by Peter, who also gets on the mic. Mainly, though, he's playing his guitar off against his amp, back often to the audience while he crafts the warp and woof of that feedback into something otherworldly. It's gloriously chaotic, veering towards their old-school shambolic ways, but it holds together, and as one of the last visual records of the band live, it packs a poignant punch.[6]

Wheels of industry

For much of the 1980s, Flying Nun would expand its local roster and international reach. The Chills were the first band on the label to tour the UK in 1985, the year Roger also went over to represent Flying Nun, meeting many of those significant indie label inspirations, such as Geoff Travis from Rough Trade, among others. This was a watershed year for Flying Nun and its artists. There was airplay on high-profile radio programmes in the UK, European international distributors were getting on board and the same was happening in the United States. Its first retrospective compilation, *Tuatara* (1985), was a hit internationally, and, as a taster from a label many had only a passing knowledge of, was a welcome showcase for bands old and new and gave listeners outside of Aotearoa a glimpse into independent music from the other side of the world.

Changes were looming, however. 1988 saw the closure of the last vinyl pressing plant in New Zealand, with the shuttering of EMI's operation in Wellington. Flying Nun now needed an overseas option to press its new releases or repress the back catalogue. Australia was the clear option, but a small label operating from a distance across the ditch risked ending up at the bottom of the pecking order.[7] To ensure an adequate and stable manufacturing and distribution deal, particularly one that could service the ever-expanding overseas interest in the label's releases and its widening import wing, Flying Nun signed on with WEA. This necessitated the label relocate from Christchurch to Auckland, the country's music industry hub, to look after the new arrangement with greater scrutiny. The informal grassroots approach of the label's earlier days did not easily scale up as its batch of artists and distribution network expanded. The financial situation, tenuous from the start, had become increasingly precarious and untenable by the decade's end. In 1989, Flying Nun was effectively insolvent. The Australian-based Mushroom Records stepped in and took on a controlling interest. In the early 1990s, Mushroom expanded to London, and Roger would shortly resettle there to look after Flying Nun's interests in Europe. With further industry mergers and acquisitions, Roger resigned from Flying Nun by the decade's end.[8]

The situation for the label and its roster afterwards is the all-too-common story of an indie label caught up in the indifferent, bottom-line machinations of an international multi-media conglomerate, where bridges are burned, back catalogues get lost or forgotten and masters mislaid (as Ben Howe discovered). There is something of a redemptive happy ending here, however. In 2009, Roger bought back the Flying Nun catalogue with the help of Neil Finn (of Split Enz and Crowded House) and others. The label slowly reconstituted itself as an independent operation, releasing new music, overseeing reissues from the back catalogue and opening brick-and-mortar shops in Auckland, Wellington (where Roger now lives), and in 2024, in a full circle moment, Christchurch.

Success story

In 2017, The Clean were honoured with the Taite Music Prize for Independent Music NZ Classic Record for *Boodle*. That same year, they were also inaugurated into the New Zealand Music Hall of Fame and awarded the APRA (Australasian Performing Rights Association) Legacy Silver Scroll Award. They had declined the offer twice before. 'The first time we lost the invite', says Robert.[9] The second time around, they stuck to their guns and insisted they would only accept if it were presented to them in Dunedin. Scott also notes a more principled reason: The Clean existed and succeeded outside of the mainstream music industry and, he says, 'in the past, we were shunned and dismissed, and it seems like by saying yes we would be forgiving the industry for that'. 'Of course', he points out, 'with time they were proved wrong as our music has stood the test of time'.[10] Hamish also made clear his disdain for these kinds of plaudits:

> What is an award? A piece of wood, plastic or metal that says you're the best and a place in some imagined hall, is the hall a vortex, does it go into infinity? Are you remembered on a black velvet painting? I really don't know what it is. I personally don't need a pat on the back.[11]

With the event finally being hosted outside of Auckland, this time at the Dunedin Town Hall, the band relented, entered the vortex and accepted the award. They did so primarily to honour the memory of Peter Gutteridge, who'd passed away in 2014, and was being inducted that year as a member of The Clean (previous invitations excluded him). This was a much more local affair, with their old friend Shayne Carter acting as musical director. On the night, a video tribute featured Gutteridge and others offering their praise and reminisces of the band. A supergroup featuring Astro Children (with Millie Lovelock on guitar and vocals), Lucy Hunter and New Zealand guitar legend Billy TK did a live cover of 'Getting Older'. Poet and friend of The Clean, David Merritt, introduced them. He proffered some pointed remarks about their cultural significance and how the industry, now honouring them, pretty much ignored them from day one:

> For The Clean to be inducted tonight, it's an important act not only of recognition by their peers and contemporaries but it's finally a small and grudging acceptance by the industry of a curious branch of the New Zealand music family, a strange distant cousin that you never had much to do with when you were younger but somehow over time they made their own communities and circles of creative talent in a town far away from Auckland, called Dunedin. I don't believe we're just awarding some gongs to The Clean here tonight. I think we are acknowledging their branch of the New Zealand music family, which we now know historically as the Dunedin Sound, a brand new at the time but a curious combo of jangly pop, strange tempos, and deeply felt attitudes. It's an aesthetic and it's an approach that owes more than a passing nod to the heritage of the late 70s and the early 80s of just do-it-yourself of lo-fi recordings and a punk-rock attitude that said 'just get on with it'.[12]

Punctuated with cries from the audience of 'stick it to the man', which he echoed in turn, Merritt's tribute is a sincere paean to the band's DIY ethic. He stressed The Clean's lack of pretension, the humble outsiders guided by an unwavering commitment to creative and musical independence in Aotearoa, and he hailed their part in making doing your thing a thing worth doing.

Beatnik

Sadly, Hamish passed away at the end of 2022. His good friend Richard Langston remembers him in a fitting tribute, one of many published in the *Pull Down The Shades* collection:

> The measure of the life is in what he created and how he influenced the culture. His impact was monumental; he altered the cultural landscape. He's there at the foundation of indie rock, and indie rock was way better for his presence. His was a brave life. It had its rewards, and it had its costs. He exasperated people at times, especially those closest to him; he could be uncompromising. But the ledger is in his and our favour. He was the multi-coloured outsider who crossed into popular culture and left us much to be inspired by, to remember to live a little more adventurously, more creatively, and to remember to always *turn it up*.[13]

You can hear that indomitable bohemian élan in his many thoughtful musings about making music, and being creative in Aotearoa. It's a legacy that comes through in one of his last recorded efforts with The Sundae Painters. This brought him together with long-standing musical comrades: Paul Kean (from Toy Love and The Bats, and who had recorded that live version of 'Platypus', the B-side to 'Tally Ho!'), Kaye Woodward (also from The Bats) and Alec Bathgate (his musical ally from The Enemy). The band produced a single and a self-titled album, both of which play psychedelia off folk, melodies off distortion, with songs couched in a warm reverb that mirrors the energy emanating from old friends easing into an exploratory jam session limned by pop contours.

Linger longer

Boodle is more than just a souvenir of its time. The Clean and their ilk were making music unheard by most of the punters in New Zealand pubs and bars, let alone on radio. Many involved in the scene then were content with that, wilfully toiling away at a margin of which they were very much the stewards. In the minds of several of these musicians, new upstart labels, and their fans, the New Zealand music industry, accountable to the multi-national majors, had been long spinning its wheels, bogged down in mundane rock and pop, ignoring artists who didn't meet (or care to meet) their need for polished and palatable sounds. Middle New Zealand, it was assumed by publicans and radio programmers, was happily accustomed to the tried/tired-and-true tunes of cover bands that soundtracked nights down at the local or middle-of-the-road hits pumped through mainstream airwaves. With the success of *Boodle*, The Clean and their contemporaries suggested otherwise, auguring in a swapping-out of the old for the new. Even if those initial forays were only incremental, they would eventually amount to a substantive changing of the guard.

Boodle anticipated and influenced a new wave of sounds and attitudes that redefined music-making in Aotearoa and overseas. While the band and Flying Nun didn't exist in a cultural vacuum (there were, as noted, other similarly inclined bands and labels around the country), *Boodle* became totemic, more so talismanic, a charismatically rough-hewn harbinger of change for the country's music industry and institutions. Having no affiliation with major labels, eschewing their distribution and promotional arms and wanting little to do with commercial radio, in skirting around the mainstream and its market logic, *Boodle*, The Clean and Flying Nun catalysed a from-the-ground-up re-imagining of how to make DIY, independent music. Playing out at first in Aotearoa, those sounds and attitudes later proved highly influential to overseas artists and labels.

In a small, sparsely populated country like New Zealand, successes tend to be writ large relative to its size. 'World famous in New Zealand' is a saying that pithily sums this up, a cheeky expression that at once modestly celebrates the local while also cautioning people to keep things humble or otherwise run the risk of being cut down, becoming a victim of 'tall-poppy syndrome'. This latter national affliction is a means of policing that modesty. In a country that imagines itself a laid-back, egalitarian democracy (another myth), no one should get too big for their britches or rise above their station. The affection for and proliferation of success stories can just as quickly lead to their exhaustion with fans and audiences, a fickleness driven by media and critics alike looking to bolster the next big thing. In shunning the rules of the game altogether, opting to invent their own as they went along, The Clean dodged ever confirming this cliché. Ignored by the mainstream media and recording industry, they did things on their terms, 'just getting on with it', making music together only when inclination and circumstance aligned. They weren't interested in the baubles of success or industry accolades; their ambitions lay elsewhere. The Clean remained content, as Robert quipped, 'quite happily going along doing our stuff'.[14] All the while sticking it to the man.

Draw(i)n(g) to a (w)hole

In January 2024, the Dunedin City Council unveiled their recent central city upgrade. Inscribed on portions of the revamped George Street, one of the city's major thoroughfares, were quotes from notable local writers and artists on the pedestrian pathway, including Janet Frame, Peter Olds and Hone Tuwhare. And, in what might be read as a poetic corrective to the Ed Sheeran slight, they also etched some of Hamish's *Boodle* lyrics: 'Anything could happen, and it could be right now. And the choice is yours, so make it worthwhile'.[15] Suitably optimistic and encouraging for a public roadway, they're written just a stone's throw from the Old Beneficiaries Hall, where The Clean had their first gig. Perhaps more than any other song on the EP, that attitude sums up the legacy of *Boodle*. By dint of historical circumstance, 'Anything Could Happen' took on an anthemic tinge by tapping into a collective sentiment, giving that feeling some structure in the form of a catchy leftfield pop song. In 1981, many in New Zealand felt the country was teetering on a bleak precipice. Better perhaps, the song advocates, to lay claim to that existential brink as a vantage point from which to plot a different course, aim towards new horizons of possibility and sort out how to make the most of what ensues. With

Boodle Boodle Boodle and everything it riled up, and all that was realized in its wake, The Clean lived this as their motto, casting off into the uncharted, channelling their creative energies to forge a singular way forward, navigating through it all by just doing their thing.

Notes

Introduction

1 Aotearoa, the te reo Māori name for the country, is used interchangeably with New Zealand throughout. Chapter and section titles are song titles from The Clean's discography.

2 https://twitter.com/benmackey/status/1535011216082739200; https://www.newshub.co.nz/home/entertainment/2022/06/clarke-gayford-not-impressed-as-ardern-and-albanese-swap-vinyl-records.html

3 Pavement covered 'Odditty' for a tribute album to the band, *God Save The Clean* (Flying Nun, 1998). The compilation includes several '90s-era US-based indie artists, such as Barbara Manning, Calexico and Guided by Voices, alongside a selection of NZ artists, all of whom have cited the band as an influence. Superchunk's Mac McCaughan and Laura Ballance founded the long-standing indie label Merge Records, which currently looks after The Clean's back catalogue and oversaw the reissues of *Boodle* and several of their albums. Yo La Tengo toured with the band, and members later appeared on The Clean's album *Getaway* (Flying Nun/Matador/Merge, 2001).

4 See *Te Ara: Encyclopedia of New Zealand*, https://teara.govt.nz/files/g-23512-data_1.txt.

5 Schmidt 2013b.

6 Barthes 1972 [1957], 143.

7 Ibid., 132.

Chapter 1

1 Robert Scott (henceforth RS), personal correspondence, 27 March 2023.

2 For more on this, see Harris 2004.

3 Staff, *Variety* 1981.

4 *Pākehā* is the te reo Māori term for foreigner, used most often, but not exclusively, to refer to European settlers and immigrants.

5 The documentary *Patu!* (Merata Mita, 1983) consists of footage shot before, during and after the protests, primarily from the organizers' point of view. Internal critiques of the organizers, mainly the Pākehā blindness to local racism regarding both Māori and Pasifika, are also vital features of the film. For a nuanced look at politics around allowing the Springboks to tour New Zealand, see McDougall 2018.

6 McNeilly 2018c.

7 For more on this, see Raymond Williams 1958a and 1961.

8 See Williams 1958b. For a read of Williams in the context of Aotearoa, see the special issue of *The Journal of New Zealand Studies* (2018), Kono, McNeill and Murray, eds.

9 As the nation's founding document, written in both te reo Māori and English and signed in 1840 by representatives of the Crown and nearly all the Māori chiefs, Te Tiriti established a relationship between the Crown and Māori, primarily regarding who had sovereignty and authority over the land. How these two concepts were (mis)translated, (mis)understood and then applied by the Crown against Māori claims to their land, over which they have never ceded sovereignty, led to the land wars in the nineteenth century and institutionalized an inequality that fuelled the strife that continues in various forms through to today. The 1975 *hīkoi* and the occupation of Takaparawhau/Bastion Point in 1978 were Māori-led protests engaging with the legacy of that conflicted interpretation of Te Tiriti. For more on this, see Ranginui Walker 2004.

10 Lawn 2004, 126.

11 Olssen 1984, 233.

12 Ibid., 243.

13 See Spittle, 'The Original Dunedin Sound, 1966–1970' and Cammick, 'Mother Goose'.

14 David Kilgour (henceforth DK), personal correspondence, 16 March 2023.

15 Ibid.

16 Ibid.

17 Sweetman 2012b.

18 For more on the history of countercultures in Aotearoa, see Nick Bollinger 2022.

19 DK, personal correspondence.

20 Colbert 1981a.

21 Radio With Pictures, *Friends of the Enemy (FotE)*, 1982.

22 The Enemy never officially released any studio recordings during their short career. However, tracks appear on various bootlegs and anthologies, including *AK 79* (Ripper Records, 1979). Some of their songs were later recorded by Toy Love and appear on that band's only studio LP, *Toy Love* (WEA, 1980).

23 Cited in Schmidt 2013c.

24 *FotE.*

25 Ibid.

26 Higgins 1982, 13.

27 Ibid.

28 Hamish Kilgour (henceforth HK), bFM. Doug Hood's long-standing and significant contributions to music in Aotearoa are detailed here: https://www.audioculture.co.nz/articles/doug-hoods-kaleidoscope-world.

29 HK, *OTD* 1979.

30 RS, personal correspondence.

31 Ibid.

32 Langston 2023a.

33 Ibid.

34 Downes, 2007. 'Scarfies' is the nickname given to students at Otago University because of the prevalent wearing of scarves, including inside their notoriously cold and damp flats. It was also the name of a 1999 film directed by Robert Sarkies that marked the film debut of Taika Waititi. It included music by many Flying Nun bands, primarily those associated with the 'Dunedin Sound', including The Clean (who made a cameo, without Hamish, playing 'Tally Ho!'), Look Blue Go Purple, and The Chills, among others. 'Bogan' is often used as a pejorative to describe a class of people assumed to be uneducated, prone to violence and with unrefined taste in clothes and culture. The term is usually associated with working-class males, thought to exhibit unsophisticated character traits, such as driving Valiants with 'fluffy dice'.

35 DK, personal correspondence.

36 Langston 2023a, 13.

37 Ibid. 'Bodgies' is a subculture of note found in both Australia and New Zealand. The term describes a group of males (the

women were referred to as 'widgies') like the UK 'rockers'. Like their British counterparts, they were associated with motorcycles, leather jackets, rock music and nicking their look from James Dean. They were the subject of many moral panics in Australia and New Zealand in the 1950s and early 1960s. They are often described as New Zealand's first gangs. They were sometimes referred to as 'milk-bar cowboys', as this was the place they'd most often congregate to listen to music and dance. They slowly evolved into 'rockers' in the 1960s, and that subculture carries on in various revivalist forms. Bodgies anticipates 'bogan' as a classed marker of social distinction.

38 RS, personal correspondence.

39 The Knobz song 'Culture?' was a response to Muldoon's comments about efforts to remove a 40 per cent sales tax on music sales in New Zealand, which was devastating the market. Muldoon refused to have it lifted, remarking that '(t)he records that are sold in this country are not Kiri Te Kanawa's: they are about 50 to one of these horrible pop groups and I'm not going to take the tax off them', *The Press*, 21 April 1980, 1. For more on the sales tax, see McLennan 2015.

40 RS, personal correspondence.

41 A history of The Empire and its role as a central venue for the Dunedin scene is outlined by Richard Langston 2015.

42 RS, personal correspondence.

43 Colbert 1981a.

44 *Ibid.*

45 Ibid.

46 Since the early 1970s, the Gladstone has been a stalwart supporter of New Zealand bands and a central institution for the country's up-and-coming bands, including its punk and post-punk artists. See Russell Brown 2013.

47 Shepherd 2016, 58.

48 DK 2015.

49 For more on making 'Tally Ho!', see Kilgour 2015; Goody 2022, 6–13.

50 Shepherd 2016, 60.

51 Colbert 1981a.

52 DK 2015.

53 McNeil 2014; Behr 2022.

54 Shepherd 2016, 60.

55 *Rip It Up* was a free monthly music magazine that started in 1977. It was central to the growth of New Zealand's independent rock and pop music cultures. It ceased publishing in 2015. For more, see Cammick 2014.

56 DK 2015.

57 DK, personal correspondence.

Chapter 2

1   DK, personal correspondence.

2   Ibid.

3   Moses 2022.

4   Ibid.

5   RS, personal correspondence.

6   Ibid.

7   Bob Sutton, personal correspondence 17 May 2024.

8   RS, personal correspondence.

9   Ibid.

10   Ibid.

11   RS, Radio Hauraki interview, 16 November 1981.

12   Langston 2023b, 14.

13   Ibid.

14   Shepherd 2016, 68.

15   RS, personal interview, 23 April 2023.

16   RS, personal correspondence.

17   Sweetman 2012b.

18   Sweetman 2012a, 43.

19   Sweetman 2012b.

20   Ibid.

21   Ibid.

22   Stanton, 13.

23   RS, personal correspondence.

24   Downes 2007.

25   Langston 2023b, 9.

26   bFM 2012b.

27   RS, personal correspondence.

28   Moses 2022.

29   DK, personal correspondence.

30   *Heavenly Pop Hits* (*HPH*).

31   Ibid.

32   RS, personal correspondence.

33   Ibid.

34   *HPH*.

35   *The Wire* 2008.

36   For a broad history of lo-fi in relation to DIY, from skiffle to riot grrrl, see Spencer 2008.

37 Russell 2012.

38 Knox in King 2008.

39 Moses 2022.

40 RS, personal correspondence.

41 Ibid.

42 Carol Tippet, personal correspondence, 28 May 2024.

43 Ibid.

44 DK, personal correspondence.

45 After initial print runs of *Boodle* with the comic were exhausted, reissues were repressed *sans* comic. Merge Records oversaw the 2021 40th anniversary reissue and remaster, with the comic restored. Currently, first pressings with the comic of the EP go for high-dollar amounts: https://www.discogs.com/release/792362-The-Clean-Boodle-Boodle-Boodle

Chapter 3

1 Schmidt 2013a.

2 Colbert 1981b.

3 Harris 2014.

4 Moses 2022.

5 Flying Nun Newsletter #2 (1982).

6 Shepherd 2016, 137.

7 Ibid., 201.

8 Day 2000, 290. A permanent radio station at Otago University, Radio One, was established in 1984. Other student stations at the time included Campus Radio B (University of Auckland, est. 1969), Radio U (University of Canterbury, Christchurch, est. 1976), Radio Active (Victoria University of Wellington, est. 1976), Contact (University of Waikato, Hamilton, est. 1977) and Radio Control (Massey University, Palmerston North, est. 1980). The slow pace at which these stations were granted permanent licences had much to do with the efforts of the two existing commercial stations, Radio Hauraki and Radio i, which contested the stations' appeals to the government to grant them longer or permanent transmitting permits. For more on this and the mythmaking around Hauraki, see Mollgaard 2012. For more on student radio in New Zealand, see Mollgaard and Neill 2023; Joyce 2021; Saw 2014.

9   Ibid.

10 The opening titles for *Grunt Machine* give a flavour of the show: https://www.nzonscreen.com/title/grunt-machine-opening-titles-1975.

11 *Radio with Pictures* occupies a contentious place in the history of music television. A selection of sources claim that, while in New Zealand in the mid-70s, Mike Nesmith, formerly of The Monkees, caught an episode of *RWP* and this eventually led to his *PopClips*, a clip show aired on Nickelodeon, and which inspired MTV. This may or may not be apocryphal. As Lee Borrie notes, Nesmith doesn't recall ever seeing *RWP*, but other sources, including MTV's Wikipedia page, make the case but with no proper attributions. See Borrie 2018.

12 Borrie 2019.

13 See, for example, McLaren's "Dots" (1940): https://youtu.be/E3-vsKwQ0Cg?si=PgxtxC7BuNIjZBBP, or Lye's "Colour Cry" from 1952: https://www.youtube.com/watch?v=2nsxTOF8V7w&list=PLq3C9x-AqtttS2-XkZFH_lIUebygqu0HO.

14 Shaw, personal interview, 23 May 2023.

15 Ibid.

16 RS, personal correspondence.

17 DK, personal correspondence.

18 RS, personal correspondence.

19 Ibid.

20 White 1982, np.

21 The Fall were local darlings for many. The Clean were certainly fans, and their impact on Flying Nun was substantial, certainly in terms of influence, but more so in ways that nearly ended the label. It was to be the first international release on the label, in the form of a live album, *Fall in a Hole*, recorded at one of their Auckland gigs. However, it all unravelled in grim fashion. For more on this, see Goody 2023 and Shepherd 2016.

22 For the full interview, see Cubey 1982.

23 *FotE*.

24 For more on *Dunedin Double*, see Smithies 2007, 62–5.

25 *Tuatara* (Flying Nun, 1985), liner notes.

26 RS, personal correspondence.

Chapter 4

1 Phillipps, cited in Mills 2016.

2 Born 2005, 8, footnote 1. Born is drawing from the work of Gilles Deleuze and Paul Rabinow and their use of the term with regard to, respectively, Foucault and technology.

3 Roger makes the claim in the 2002 documentary, *Heavenly Pop Hits*; for David's utterance, see Maclennan 1981, 6. For more on this, see Robertson, 121-139.

4   Downes 2011, 43.

5   See https://www.youtube.com/watch?v=OhKsp2621kA.

6   On 'liveness' and The Clean, see Jorgensen 2017.

7   Dix 1988, 250.

8   Kay 1986, 16.

9   DK, personal correspondence.

10   RS, personal correspondence.

11   Carter 2019, 135.

12   Kilroy on RNZ 2022.

13   For an autobiographical counternarrative to those that otherwise lionize the Dunedin Sound, see Matthew Bannister 1999.

14   Holland and Wilson 2015, np.

15   Downes 2011, 43.

16   This is a play on Michael Billig's 'banal nationalism'. See Billig 1995.

17   Bannister 2019, 60–1.

18   For more on the myth of isolation, see Schmidt 2016.

19   Aston 2009.

20   An obvious nod to the Dunedin Sound, the Wellington Sound was occasionally used to refer to a particular scene in the country's capital city from the early-to-mid-2000s, a mix of dub, reggae, hip-hop, Polynesian soul and dance music. For a humorous take, and his complicity in it, see Grant Smithies 2006.

21   Williamson 2010.

22   McLeay 1994, 44.

23   Ibid., 45.

24   Ibid., 46–7.

Chapter 5

1   Richard Ley-Hamilton, cited in McNeilly 2014.

2   Centre Negative, excerpt from the track 'In', from the album *Emotion Is Cringey* (Melted Ice Cream, 2015).

3   McConnell 2018.

4   Gibb 2018.

5   McNeilly 2018c.

6   For more on neoliberalism and its impact in New Zealand, see Kelsey 2015.

7   Franklin 1985, 22–6.

8   Gluckman 2014, np.

9   Johansson and Kociatkiewicz 2011, 392.

10 In 2014, Dunedin became the first UNESCO Creative City in Aotearoa (explicitly designated as City of Literature). See https://en.unesco.org/creative-cities/dunedin.

11 Löfgren 2003, 244.

12 *A Spatial Plan for Dunedin*, 08.

13 Otago Arts Festival, np.

14 Patterson 2018.

15 Benson 2011.

16 Staff, *Mix* 2022a.

17 For more on the Dead C, including the band's relationship with Flying Nun, see Darren Jorgensen (2023) on their album, *Clyma est Mort*.

18 Lewis 2012.

19 Colbert, in Loughrey 2014.

20 See Howe 2018.

21 Michael Brown 2018. See also Brown 2019.

22 Mills 2020, 26.

23 See https://www.otago.ac.nz/library/hocken/exhibitions/
    kaleidoscope-world-forty-years-of-flying-nun. *Kaleidoscope
    World* (Flying Nun, 1986) is the title of a compilation
    album from The Chills. Both the Hocken and the Turnbull
    are affiliated with the Flying Nun Foundation (https://
    flyingnunfoundation.net). A registered charity, it consists
    of people 'who are part of the story and who have come
    together to ensure that the heritage of the Flying Nun label
    is preserved, safely stored, catalogued and accessible'. They
    aim to advise private holders of any label-related materials,
    from recordings to posters to videos, and act as a bridge
    connecting individuals to the institutions dotting the
    country with Flying Nun materials already in their collections.

24 Lewis 2022.

25 See *Ōtepoti Live Music Action Plan*, Dunedin City Council, 43.

26 Lindner 2006, 55.

27 McNeilly 2018b.

28 Staff, Ōtepoti Gig Guides, *Dunedinsound.com* 2018.

29 Oliver 2018.

30 Herchenbach 2021. Herchenbach had an ally in this: A caveat
    in the *Hellzapoppin'* catalogue notes that The Clean declined
    to include any of their art and design in the retrospective.
    See Christchurch City Gallery 2021, 92.

31 Lindner 2006, 58.

32 Ibid.

33 Steel 2016.

34 Barthes 1972 [1957], 132.

Chapter 6

1 HK, 2015.

2 The individual members remained musically active. Hamish
and David would join up with original Clean member Peter
Gutteridge in The Great Unwashed (which also included
Ross Humphries from The Pin Group), a more acoustic,
psychedelia-inclined outing, which spawned singles and an
LP, *Clean Out of Our Minds* (Flying Nun, 1983). Robert formed
The Bats (with Toy Love member Paul Kean, alongside Kaye
Woodward and Malcolm Grant), which continues to record
and tour. He was also involved with The Weeds and Magick
Heads, among others, and has several solo releases. David
had a brief stint in The Chills, and he later formed Stephen,
which released an EP, *Dumb* (1988) and one LP, *Radar of Small
Dogs* (Flying Nun, 1993). He also carried on solo, with releases
like *Here Come The Cars* (Flying Nun, 1991), *Sugar Mouth*
(Flying Nun, 1994) and more. He also made several albums
accompanied by The Heavy Eights, including a collaboration
with poet Sam Hunt, *Falling Debris* (Arch Hill, 2008). He was
the subject of the documentary *Far Off Town – Dunedin to
Nashville* (Bridget Sutherland, 2006), which captures his visit
to Nashville to work with his friends in the band Lambchop,
among other artists. David was made a Member of the New
Zealand Order of Merit for services to music in 2001. Hamish
was Flying Nun's first paid employee in 1982, packing and
posting records (among other tasks). He co-founded Bailter
Space and played on their debut LP, *Tanker* (Flying Nun,
1988), and a selection of singles. On tour with the band
through the United States, he stayed on in New York, where
he formed The Mad Scene. They released a few singles and a

handful of albums, including *A Trip Thru Monsterland* (Flying Nun, 1993) and *Sealight* (Little Teddy Recordings, 1995). He later put out some solo records: *All of It and Nothing* (Ba Da Bing!, 2014), *Finklestein* (Ba Da Bing!, 2018) and *Franklestein* (Ba Da Bing!, 2019). Over the years, Hamish played with Australian band The Moles, Christchurch compatriot Bill Direen, Yo La Tengo, Dean Wareham/Luna, Tall Dwarfs, Auckland outfit Tiny Ruins, and many others. All three Clean members also maintained their non-musical creative output through painting, drawing, and more.

3   RS, personal correspondence; See also the Chill Blue (2019) interview clip from the UK in 1990, following the release of *Vehicle*.

4   Christgau 1990.

5   The Clean, 'Point That Thing Live,' *YouTube*. 31 January 2014. https://youtu.be/7uHHVQnd7vM?si=sS4l1BUM3vt5co_K

6   One of the most well-known live versions of 'Point That Thing' was recorded by Bob Sutton at a gig The Clean did at the Rumba Bar in Auckland, in November of 1981, in support of *Boodle*. https://www.youtube.com/watch?v=mCkLuizMwlU. Clocking in at fifteen minutes, it has them at their noisiest best, at the end of which an unsatiated fan urges 'Do it again!'.

7   Shepherd 2016, 176.

8   Roger details much of this tumultuous period in the latter half of his autobiography.

9   RS, *RNZ* 2017a.

10 Anderson 2017.

11 Ibid.

12 David Merritt *RNZ* 2017b.

13 Langston 2023a, 274. See also tributes in *The Guardian* (https://www.theguardian.com/music/2022/dec/06/hamish-kilgour-co-founder-of-new-zealand-band-the-clean-dies-aged-65), *New York Times* (https://www.nytimes.com/2022/12/09/arts/music/hamish-kilgour-dead.html), *NPR* (https://www.npr.org/2022/12/06/1140939082/obituary-hamish-kilgour-the-clean) and *Rolling Stone* (https://www.rollingstone.com/music/music-news/hamish-kilgour-new-zealand-indie-the-clean-dead-1234641744/) all of which pay homage to Hamish's impact on independent musicmaking in New Zealand and internationally.

14 RS, personal interview.

15 Cited by McNeilly 2024.

Works Cited

95 bFM (2012a). 'Extended Play: The Clean – Hamish Kilgour'. *YouTube*. 12 March. https://youtu.be/8NEbKYbDMqA?si=RbYa Ed2x800CM2J-

95 bFM (2012b). 'Extended Play: The Clean – Boodle Boodle Boodle'. 27 April. https://youtu.be/sTk4gM5Dbts?si=u5dixooZ gkBqvSx-

Anderson, V. (2017). 'Silver Scrolls: Anything Could Happen at this Year's Dunedin Ceremony'. *Stuff*. 27 September. https://www. stuff.co.nz/entertainment/music/97297700/silver-scrolls-anything-could-happen-at-this-years-dunedin-ceremony

Aston, M. (2009). 'Nuns at the Altar of Rock: Flying Nun Records'. *The Guardian*. 15 May. https://www.theguardian.com/music/2009/may/15/flying-nun-indie-rought-trade

Bannister, M. (1999). *Positively George Street: A Personal History of Sneaky Feelings and the Dunedin Sound*. Auckland: Reed.

Bannister, M. (2019). 'Not Given Lightly: Chris Knox, Nationalism, Whiteness and Punk/Indie Discourse in Aotearoa/New Zealand'. *Perfect Beat*, 20 (1): 40–67.

Barthes, R. (1972 [1957]). *Mythologies*. Trans. Annette Lavers. New York: Farrar, Straus & Giroux.

Behr, A. (2022). '? and the Mysterians' "96 Tears"'. *One-Hit Wonders: An Oblique History of Popular Music*. Hill, S. (Ed.). New York: Bloomsbury Publishing USA. 21–8.

Benson, N. (2011). '"Dunedin Sound" Album Toasted in Unique Style'. *Otago Daily Times*. 9 April. https://www.odt.co.nz/news/dunedin/dunedin-sound-album-toasted-unique-style

Billig, M. (1995). *Banal Nationalism*. London: Sage.

Bollinger, N. (2022). *Jumping Sundays: The Rise and Fall of the Counterculture in Aotearoa New Zealand*. Auckland: Auckland University Press.

Born, G. (2005). 'On Musical Mediation: Ontology, Technology and Creativity'. *Twentieth-Century Music*, 2 (1): 7–36.

Borrie, L. (2018). 'Radio with Pictures: Pt. 1'. *Audioculture*. 13 June. https://www.audioculture.co.nz/articles/radio-with-pictures-an-oral-history-part-one

Borrie, L. (2019). 'Radio with Pictures: Pt. 3'. *Audioculture*. 21 November. https://www.audioculture.co.nz/articles/radio-with-pictures-history-3

Brown, M. (2018). 'Flying Nun Records: Collection'. *National Library of New Zealand*. July. https://natlib.govt.nz/blog/posts/atl100-new-collections#FlyingNun

Brown, M. (2019). 'The Flying Nun Project: Tally Ho!' *National Library of New Zealand*. 8 May. https://natlib.govt.nz/blog/posts/the-flying-nun-project-tally-ho

Brown, R. (2013). 'The Gladstone Hotel'. *Audioculture*. 22 August. https://www.audioculture.co.nz/articles/the-gladstone-hotel

Cammick, M. (2013). 'Mother Goose'. *Audioculture*. 19 April. https://www.audioculture.co.nz/profile/mother-goose

Cammick, M. (2014). 'Rip It Up'. *Audioculture*. 21 May. https://www.audioculture.co.nz/articles/rip-it-up

Carter, S. (2019). *Dead People I Have Known*. Wellington: Victoria University Press.

Chapman, I. (2016). *The Dunedin Sound: Some Disenchanted Evening*. Auckland: Bateman.

Chill Blue (2019). 'The Clean: Interview in UK 1990'. *YouTube*. 30 December. https://www.youtube.com/watch?v=ou4C_3g_RoE

Christchurch Art Gallery (2021). *Hellzapoppin'!: The Art of Flying Nun*. Christchurch: Australian Book Connection.

Christgau, R. (1990). 'The Clean'. *Robertchristgau.com*. https://www.robertchristgau.com/get_artist.php?id=1401

Colbert, R. (1981a). 'Clean "Tally Ho"'. *Rip It Up*, 50. 1 September, 8.

Colbert, R. (1981b). 'The Clean: Boodle'. *Rip It Up*, 52. 1 November, 26.

Corlett, E. (2022). 'Ardern's Fiancé Takes Swipe at Albanese's Outdated Music Taste after Leaders Exchange Records'. *The Guardian*. 10 June. https://www.theguardian.com/music/2022/jun/10/arderns-fiancee-takes-swipe-at-albaneses-outdated-music-taste-after-leaders-exchange-records

Cubey, M. (1982). 'The Fall, Union Hall August 19'. *Salient*. 6 September. https://thefall.org/news/fallnz.html

Day, P. (2000). *Voice and Vision: A History of Broadcasting in New Zealand, Vol. 2*. Auckland: Auckland University Press.

Dix, J. (1988). *Stranded in Paradise: New Zealand Rock'n'Roll 1955–1988*. Auckland: Paradise Publications.

Downes, G. (2007). 'Singing G against the E Chord'. *Public Address*. 19 November. https://publicaddress.net/speaker/singing-g-against-the-e-chord/

Downes, G. (2009). 'Singing G against the E Chord'. *Public Address*. 19 November. https://publicaddress.net/speaker/singing-g-against-the-e-chord/

Downes, G. (2011). 'Songwriting Process in the Verlaines' Album *Corporate Moronic*. *Dunedin Soundings: Place and Performance*. Bendrups, D., & Downes, G. (Eds.). Dunedin: Otago University Press. 43–56.

Dunedin City Council (2024). *Ōtepoti Live Music Action Plan*. 19 March. https://www.dunedin.govt.nz/services/arts-and-culture/otepoti-live-music-action-plan

Franklin, S. H. (1985). *Cul de Sac: The Question of New Zealand's Future*. Auckland: Unwin Paperbacks.

Gibb, J. (2018). 'Ed Sheeran Concerts to Be Marked with Mural'. *Otago Daily Times*. 9 March. https://www.odt.co.nz/news/dunedin/ed-sheeran-concerts-be-marked-mural

Gluckman, P. (2014). 'Foreword'. *No. 8 Re-Wired: 202 New Zealand Inventions That Changed the World*. Downs, D., & Bridges, J. (Eds.). Auckland: Penguin Random House New Zealand Limited. Np.

Goody, M. (2022). *Needles and Plastic: Flying Nun Records, 1981–1988*. Auckland: Auckland University Press.

Goody, M. (2023). 'Uncharted Territory: How the Fall's Fractious New Zealand Tour Nearly Sank Flying Nun Records'. *The Guardian*. 21 February. https://www.theguardian.com/music/2023/feb/21/the-fall-band-new-zealand-flying-nun-record-company

Harris, A. (2004). *Hīkoi: Forty Years of Māori Protest*. Auckland: Huia Publishers.

Harris, J. (2014). 'The Clean: I Think This Upcoming Tour Will Be Our Last'. *Tone Deaf*. 17 December. https://tonedeaf.thebrag.com/the-clean-i-think-this-upcoming-tour-will-be-our-last/

Hawkes, M. (2002). *Heavenly Pop Hits: The Flying Nun Story*. https://www.nzonscreen.com/title/heavenly-pop-hits-the-flying-nun-story-2002

Herchenbach, H. (2021). 'The ~~Dunedin~~ Christchurch Sound: A Revisionist History'. *B*. 30 August. https://christchurchartgallery.org.nz/bulletin/205/the-deldunedindel-christchurch-sound.

Higgins, M. (1982). 'Do They Have McDonald's Down There?'. *Rip It Up*. 1 April, 10–13.

Holland, M., & Wilson, O. (2015). 'Technostalgia in New Recording Projects by the 1980s "Dunedin Sound" Band The Chills'. *Journal on the Art of Record Production*, 9. https://www.arpjournal.com/asarpwp/technostalgia-in-new-recording-projects-by-the-1980s-dunedin-sound-band-the-chills/

Howe, B. (2018). 'How the Lost Flying Nun Master Tapes Found a Home'. 5 September. http://benhowe.co.nz/latest/2018/9/5/how-the-lost-flying-nun-master-tapes-found-a-home

James, C. (2015). *The Quiet Revolution: Turbulence and Transition in Contemporary New Zealand*. Auckland: Bridget Williams Books.

Johansson, M., & Kociatkiewicz, J. (2011). 'City Festivals: Creativity and Control in Staged Urban Experiences'. *European Urban and Regional Studies*, 18 (4): 392–405.

Jorgensen, D. (2017). 'Liveness and Improficiency in The Clean's Influence upon Dunedin Sound Bands'. *Perfect Beat*, 18 (2): 154–65.

Jorgensen, D. (2023). *The Dead C's Clyma est mort*. New York: Bloomsbury.

Joyce, Z. (2021). 'Student Radio: "A Good Friend of New Zealand Music"'. *Journal of Radio & Audio Media*, 28 (1): 125–43.

Kay, G. (1986). 'Feeling Sentimental: Dunedin Mon Amour'. *Rip It Up*, 113, 16.

Kelsey, J. (2015). *The FIRE Economy: New Zealand's Reckoning*. Auckland: Bridget Williams Books.

Kilqour, D. (2015). 'The Story Behind "Tally Ho"'. *Audioculture*. 16 July. https://www.audioculture.co.nz/articles/the-story-behind-tally-ho

King, B. (2008). 'Chris Knox Interview: 4 Track and Flying Nun, Part 2'. *YouTube*. https://www.youtube.com/watch?v=0i2fdfcJJBc

Kono, S., McNeill, D., & Murray, A. (Eds.) (2018). *The Journal of New Zealand Studies*. NS26.

Langston, R. (2015). 'The Empire Tavern'. *Audioculture*. 13 April. https://www.audioculture.co.nz/articles/the-empire-tavern

Langston, R. (2023a). *Pull Down the Shades – Garage Fanzine 1984–86: Tales from the New Zealand Underground*. Chicago: HoZac Books.

Langston, R. (2023b). 'The Last Retro-Show'. *Garage 6*, 7–11.

Lawn, J. (2004). 'Scarfies, Dunedin Gothic, and the Spirit of Capitalism'. *Journal of New Zealand Literature*, 22: 124–40.

Lewis, J. (2012). 'Dunedin Sound Is Now on Record at Museum'. *Otago Daily Times*. 7 December. https://www.odt.co.nz/news/dunedin/dunedin-sound-now-record-museum

Lewis, J. (2022). 'Rallying to Protect Live Music Scene'. *Otago Daily Times*, 27 July. https://www.odt.co.nz/news/dunedin/rallying-protect-live-music-scene

Lindner, R. (2006). 'The Cultural Texture of the City'. *Cities and Media: Cultural Perspectives on Urban Identities in a Mediatized World*. Conference Proceedings. https://ep.liu.se/ecp/020/005/ecp072005.pdf

Löfgren, O. (2003). 'The New Economy: A Cultural History'. *Global Networks*, 3 (3): 239–54.

Loughrey, D. (2014). 'Dunedin Sound for Sinfonia'. *Otago Daily Times*. 17 December. https://www.odt.co.nz/news/dunedin/dunedin-sound-sinfonia

Maclennan, D. (1981)."Keeping It Clean". *In Touch*, 7.

McConnell, G. (2018). 'Kiwi Musos Ask Why: Why Is the Dunedin Council Paying for an Ed Sheeran Mural?' *Stuff*. 10 March. https://www.stuff.co.nz/entertainment/arts/102148308/

kiwi-musos-ask-why-why-is-the-dunedin-council-paying-for-an-ed-sheeran-mural

McDougall, H. (2018). '"The Whole World's Watching": New Zealand, International Opinion, and the 1981 Springbok Rugby Tour'. *Journal of Sport History*, 45 (2): 202–23

McLeay, C. (1994). 'The "Dunedin Sound": New Zealand Rock and Cultural Geography'. *Perfect Beat*, 2 (1): 38–50.

McLennan, P. (2015). 'Sales Tax on LPs in 1970s NZ'. *Audioculture*. 21 May. https://www.audioculture.co.nz/articles/sales-tax-on-lps-in-1970s-nz

McNeil, L. (2014). 'Question Mark & the Mysterians Making of "96 Tears"'. *Vice*. 27 February. https://www.vice.com/en/article/jmbpdd/question-mark–the-mysterians—the-making-of-96-tears

McNeilly, H. (2014). 'Dunedin Sound Recalled'. *Otago Daily Times*. 25 July. https://www.odt.co.nz/news/dunedin/dunedin-sound-recalled

McNeilly, H. (2018a). 'Ed Sheeran Mural a "Slap in the Face" for Local Art, Dunedin Councillor suggests'. *Stuff*. 15 May. https://www.stuff.co.nz/national/103870203/ed-sheeran-mural-a-slap-in-the-face-for-local-art-dunedin-councillor-suggests

McNeilly, H. (2018b). 'Unheavenly Pop Hit: The Chills Artwork Vandalised by Other Band and Filmed'. *Otago Daily Times*. 28 February. https://www.stuff.co.nz/national/101835673/unheavenly-pop-hit-the-chills-artwork-vandalised-by-other-band-and-filmed

McNeilly, H. (2018c). 'Declassified Intelligence Service Documents Confirm New Zealand Assassination Attempt on Queen Elizabeth II'. *Stuff*. 1 March. https://www.stuff.co.nz/national/crime/101794948/the-snowman-and-the-queen-declassified-nz-intelligence-service-documents-confirm-assassination-attempt-on-queen

McNeilly, H. (2024). 'Seminal Kiwi Band Etched into Dunedin's CBD Redevelopment'. *Otago Daily Times*. 26 January. https://www.stuff.co.nz/culture/350159851/seminal-kiwi-band-etched-dunedins-cbd-redevelopment

Mills, A. (2016). 'The Dunedin Sound: The Sound of Honesty?' *Audioculture*. 15 November. https://www.audioculture.co.nz/articles/dunedin-sound-the-sound-of-honesty

Mills, A. P. (2020). 'Scene and Heard: Collecting the Dunedin Sound'. *Popular Music History*, 13: 18–37.

Mollgaard, M. (2012). 'Pirate Stories: Rethinking the Radio Rebels'. *Radio and Society: New Thinking for an Old Medium*. Mollgaard, Matt (Ed.). Cambridge: Cambridge Scholars. 51–64.

Mollgaard, M., & Neill, K. (2023). *'Other Stations Are Shit': Student Radio in Aotearoa New Zealand*. Auckland: Harvest.

Moses, H. (2022). 'An Oral History of The Clean's Boodle Boodle Boodle EP'. *The Spinoff*. 10 December. https://thespinoff.co.nz/pop-culture/10-12-2022/an-oral-history-of-the-cleans-boodle-boodle-boodle-ep.

Oliver, H. (2018). 'Astro Children: "The Only Dunedin Sound I Have Ever Cared about Is My Own"'. *Spinoff*. 9 March. https://thespinoff.co.nz/pop-culture/09-03-2018/astro-children-the-only-dunedin-sound-i-have-ever-cared-about-is-my-own

Olssen, E. (1984). *A History of Otago*. Dunedin: John McIndoe Limited.

Otago Arts Festival (2001). *Programme*. Otago Arts Festival, Dunedin. Np.

Patterson, G. (2018). 'DCC Launches "Dunedin Sound" Initiative'. *Otago Daily Times*. https://www.odt.co.nz/news/dunedin/dcc/dcc-launches-dunedin-sound-initiative

Radio with Pictures (1982). 'Friends of the Enemy'. *YouTube*. https://www.youtube.com/watch?v=NzoOBoX6TCw

RNZ (2017a). 'The Clean to Be Inducted into NZ Music Hall of Fame'. *RNZ*. 10 September. https://www.rnz.co.nz/national/programmes/sunday/audio/201857968/the-clean-to-be-inducted-into-nz-music-hall-of-fame

RNZ (2017b). 'David Merritt Inducts The Clean into the NZ Music Hall of Fame | Silver Scrolls 2017'. *YouTube*. https://www.youtube.com/watch?v=jYxFuKYt3m8

RNZ (2022). 'The Dunedin Sound with Stephen Kilroy'. *RNZ*. 2 January. https://www.rnz.co.nz/national/programmes/the-weekend/audio/2018826182/the-dunedin-sound-with-stephen-kilroy.

Robertson, C. (1991). *'It's OK, It's All Right, Oh Yeah': The 'Dunedin Sound'? An Aspect of Alternative Music in New Zealand 1978–1985*. Dunedin: BA (Hons), Otago University.

Russell, B. (2012). 'Bird-Like Antique Chatter: Mis-Competence in New Zealand Electronic Music'. *White Fungus*. https://www.whitefungus.com/history-new-zealand-diy-electronic-music

Saw, Y. (2014). 'A History of Student Radio: A Four-Part Journey through 45 Years of Student Radio in New Zealand'. *RNZ*. 27 December. https://www.rnz.co.nz/national/programmes/a-history-of-student-radio

Schmidt, A. (2013a). 'The Clean Part One 1978–1988'. *Audioculture*. 6 November. https://www.audioculture.co.nz/articles/the-clean-part-one-1978-1988.

Schmidt, A. (2013b). 'Propeller Records, the Post-Punk Evolution and the NZ Indie Boom – 1980–1983'. *Audioculture*. 23 October. https://www.audioculture.co.nz/labels/propeller

Schmidt, A. (2013c). 'The Enemy'. *Audioculture*. 16 April. https://www.audioculture.co.nz/profile/the-enemy

Schmidt, A. (2016). 'Flying Nun Records, the Dunedin Sound and the Myth of Isolation'. *Audioculture*. 7 January. https://www. audioculture.co.nz/articles/flying-nun-records-the-dunedin-sound-and-the-myth-of-isolation

Scott, R. (1981). *The Clean Interview*. Radio Hauraki. 16 November.

Shepherd, R. (2016). *In Love with These Times: My Life with Flying Nun Records*. Auckland: HarperCollins.

Smithies, G. (2006). 'A Different Beat'. *Sunday Star Times*. 5 March. supp., 16–20.

Smithies, G. (2007). *Soundtrack: 118 Great New Zealand Albums*. Auckland: Craig Potton Pub.

Spencer, A. (2008). *DIY: The Rise of Lo-Fi Culture*. London: Marion Boyars Publishers.

Spittle, G. (2013). 'The Original Dunedin Sound – 1966–1970'. *Audioculture*. 24 July. https://www.audioculture.co.nz/articles/the-original-dunedin-sound-1966-1970

Staff (1979). 'Keeping It Clean and Basic'. *Auckland Star*. 20 September. Np.

Staff (2010). 'Flying High'. *Stuff*. 23 July. https://www.stuff.co.nz/the-press/christchurch-life/art-and-stage/christchurch-music/3949260/Flying-HIGH

Staff (2018). 'Life in the Shadow of the Dunedin Sound'. *Ōtepoti Gig Guides*. 9 March. https://dunedinsound.com/blog/life_in_the_shadow_of_the_dunedin_sound/

Staff (2022a). 'New Zealand's Dunedin Sound Inspires University Music Program'. *Mix*. 21 March. https://www.mixonline.com/recording/new-zealands-dunedin-sound-inspires-university-music-program

Staff (2022b). 'Crown Hotel: March Organised to Save Iconic Dunedin Venue the Crown Hotel'. *RNZ*. 7 August. https://www.

rnz.co.nz/news/national/472385/march-organised-to-save-iconic-dunedin-venue-the-crown-hotel

Staff, B., & Ashley, S. (2002). *For the Record: A History of the Recording Industry in New Zealand*. Auckland: David Bateman.

Steel, G. (2016). 'Flying Nun: In Love with the Sound of Their Own Voice, More Like'. *The Spinoff*. 14 June. https://thespinoff.co.nz/analysis/14-06-2016/flying-nun-in-love-with-the-sound-of-their-own-voice-more-like

Sweetman, S. (2012a). *On Song: Stories behind New Zealand Pop Classics*. Auckland: Penguin.

Sweetman, S. (2012b). 'The Poppies Want to Grow a Little Taller'. *Stuff*. 19 January. https://www.stuff.co.nz/entertainment/music/6280128/The-poppies-want-to-grow-a-little-taller

Taylor, M. (2016). 'Dunedin Sound in Pictures Planned'. *Otago Daily Times*. 27 April. https://www.odt.co.nz/news/dunedin/dunedin-sound-pictures-planne

Variety Staff (1981). 'Goodbye Pork Pie'. *Variety*. 31 December. https://variety.com/1980/film/reviews/goodbye-pork-pie-1200424976/

Walker, R. (2004). *Ka Whawhai Tonu Matou/Struggle without End*. Auckland: Penguin.

White, R. (1982). 'The Clean – Who Wants Success'. *Auckland Star*, 10 June. Np.

Williams, R. (1958a). *Culture and Society, 1780–1950*. London: Chatto & Windus.

Williams, R. (1958b). 'Culture Is Ordinary'. *Conviction*. MacKenzie, Norman (Ed.). London: MacGibbon and Kee. 75.

Williams, R. (1961). *The Long Revolution*. New York: Columbia University Press.

Williamson, L. (2010). 'Flying High'. *The Press*. 23 July, 13.

Index